BOLD SEA
STORIES 2

Praise for Bold Seas Series

"…an adrenalin surge while being an inspirational look into human nature when the chips are down…"— *Soundings*

"…a fascinating read, well-researched and written with gripping true stories."— *Canadian Yachting*

"Brave and true. Marlin Bree brings a mariner's insight to 21 stories (that) capture the drama and inspiration of dealing with challenges on the water. Each of these excellent stories can be read in under an hour." — *The Ensign*

"… a knack for writing about the legends and lore of the world's wildest waters." — *Boating Writers International*

"…will keep you page-turning." — *Lake Superior Magazine*

"…true tales of storms, shipwrecks, and doomed crews fighting incredible challenges." — *Duluth News Tribune*

BOLD SEA STORIES 2

TRUE BOATING TALES OF ADVENTURE AND SURVIVAL

MARLIN BREE

MARLOR PRESS
St. Paul, Minnesota

BOLD SEA STORIES 2
Book Two in the Bold Sea Stories Series

Copyright © 2023
By MARLIN BREE

Design by Theresa Gedig/Dig Design
Edited by Patricia Morris
Published by Marlor Press, Inc

Paperback: 9781-892147-37-0
E-Book: 9781-892147-38-7

Printed in the United States of America

Distributed to the book trade in the USA by
Independent Publishers Group, Chicago

MARLOR PRESS
4304 Brigadoon Drive • Saint Paul, MN 55126

Bold Sea Stories Series
First Edition

Library of Congress Cataloging-in-Publication Data

Names: Bree, Marlin, 1933- author.
Title: Bold sea stories 2 : true boating tales of adventure and survival /
Marlin Bree.
Other titles: Bold sea stories two
Description: First edition. | St. Paul, MN : Marlor Press, [2022] | Series:
Bold sea stories series | Includes bibliographical references and index.
Identifiers: LCCN 2022044356 (print) | LCCN 2022044357 (ebook) | ISBN
9781892147370 (paperback) | ISBN 9781892147387 (ebook)
Subjects: LCSH: Sea stories. | Seafaring life. | Survival at sea. | Voyages
and travels. | Shipwrecks.
Classification: LCC G525 .B812 2023 (print) | LCC G525 (ebook) | DDC
910.4/5--dc23/eng/20221024
LC record available at https://lccn.loc.gov/2022044356
LC ebook record available at https://lccn.loc.gov/2022044357

CONTENTS

Re Read !

But in the darkest,
Meanest things,
There alway, alway
Something sings.

—RALPH WALDO EMERSON

Marlin Bree Books

BOLD SEA SERIES

Bold Sea Stories (Book One)
Bold Sea Stories 2 (Book Two)

Other books

Wake of the Green Storm

Broken Seas

In the Teeth of the Northeaster

Boat Log & Record

Call of the North Wind

Alone Against the Atlantic
(By Gerry Spiess with Marlin Bree)

Fiction

Dead on the Wind

Audiobooks

Wake of the Green Storm
In the Teeth of the Northeaster

PREFACE

The Voyage Begins

It was a hot July morning in White Bear, Minnesota, and nine-year-old Vinette was the first neighborhood kid to show up.

"What are you building now?" she asked, barely controlling her mirth. "An *airplane*?"

"It's going to be a *boat*," Gerry Spiess said, brushing a patina of sawdust from his face. Vinette chuckled.

The girl had visited his "boatyard"—the garage attached to his house—many times before, and this was their ritual: neighborhood kids vs. the amateur boatbuilder. The kids always won.

Vinette inched closer, her eyes growing wide. Gerry's building project was just ribs and a frame. It rested, upside down, on only two kitchen chairs.

"It could be a boat, I guess," she allowed. "Going to take a trip in this one?"

"You never know. Maybe someday. But for now, I'm building it just to try out some ideas. It's an experiment."

Experiment or not, it was something he had always wanted to do, and in a little under a month, his garage project grew into a ten-foot-long sailboat. Audaciously, he dunked his tiny craft into the North Atlantic and set sail eastward. *England, Ho!*

Surviving towering waves and ferocious storms, the Minnesota schoolteacher caught the world's attention after a tumultuous fifty-four-day crossing. It was a record: *Yankee Girl* was the smallest boat to cross the North Atlantic, west to east.

The resulting book we wrote, *Alone Against the Atlantic,* became a tonic for uncertain times and rose on the charts to become a national best-seller. *Readers Digest Condensed Books* published it as an "inspiring true story of one man's dream, from its birth to its glorious fulfillment."

Gerry astutely observed lessons from his harrowing voyage: "You don't go to sea to rough it," he told me. "You go to smooth it." Gerry spent a lot of time aboard his boat to make his adventure as successful as possible before taking her to the North Atlantic—sleeping, eating, and sailing on White Bear Lake. "Never go to sea in a new boat, only an 'old boat,'"

Marlin Bree and Gerry Spiess on the waterfront.

he observed. He meant a well-tried and thoroughly tested boat.

I listened carefully, not only to write the book with him but because I was building my boat. As a first-time boatbuilder, I could use all the help I could get, especially considering that *Persistence* was headed for Lake Superior. Between writing bouts around Gerry's kitchen table on Floral Avenue in White Bear, Gerry obligingly would come over to my nearby Shoreview home to inspect the hull arising in my garage. A lot of Gerry's observations went into *Persistence's* construction. In the chapter "Secrets of Survival," the advice I got paid off when my twenty-foot sloop ran afoul of "the storm of the century."

Gerry loved challenges. If you follow your dreams, he once told me, one of two things can happen: You can achieve what you want or have a great time trying.

Gerry's spirit of adventure lives on in an excerpt from *Alone Against the Atlantic* (Copyright Gerry Spiess and Marlin Bree). In "Overboard," the lone sailor runs into trouble on the raging North Atlantic—until his boat takes a hand. Coincidence? Some might call it a minor miracle.

Adventuring is not always what you have, but what you do with what you have. In "Lure of the High Ice," a boater lying at anchor in the Caribbean overhears a radio message: The infamous Northwest Passage might open up this year. Boldly, he sets sail up the Atlantic Coast, resupplying his well-traveled ketch with goods, gas, and down-home crew—and enters the icy route that doomed the Franklin Expedition.

In other chapters, tales from Lake Superior—the world's largest freshwater lake and regarded by many as an inland ocean—will whisk you to where the wild wind blows free, sometimes much too free, and take you to what lies below in its dark depths. Be prepared to shed a tear.

For example, a monstrous wooden ship lies just beyond Outer Island in the Apostle Islands. She's not only historically fascinating, but you can get down to her in only fifty-five feet of water—one of the most accessible shipwrecks. She is the largest wooden ship ever built and is a sport diver's paradise—but how did she get there? The mystery unfolds in "The Lost Ships."

One bleak morning, a lighthouse keeper is startled to see only the masts of a large sailing vessel sticking out of stormy waters. There's someone up there, and a close look with binoculars tells him that they are crewmembers who climbed the rigging, looking for salvation. But they are not moving. Covered in six inches of ice—they are frozen stiff. What went wrong? Read "Ship of Death."

Armchair adventurers can pursue true-life boating tales in a reading time of about fifteen to twenty-five minutes each. Some take more time, some less, depending on your degree of resonance and involvement. Some will keep you on edge, shiver your timbers—and maybe toss you on your emotional beam ends. That might take a little more time. Trust me.

All my stories are authentic—real boats, real people, actual events. Fact is more potent than fiction. Thank you for reading my book. Please enjoy!

—Marlin Bree, *author*
Bold Sea Series

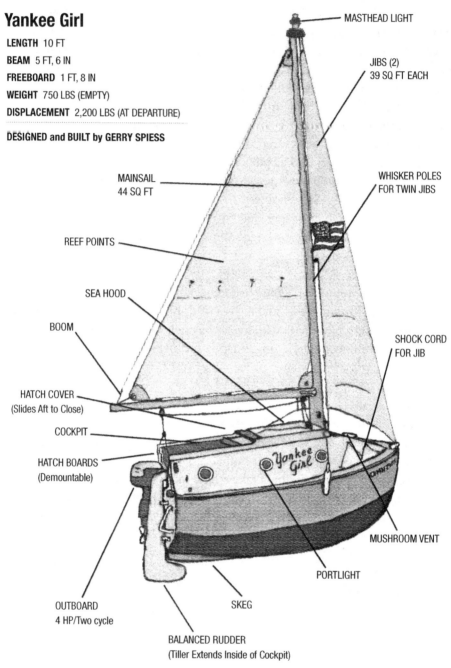

Yankee Girl

LENGTH 10 FT
BEAM 5 FT, 6 IN
FREEBOARD 1 FT, 8 IN
WEIGHT 750 LBS (EMPTY)
DISPLACEMENT 2,200 LBS (AT DEPARTURE)

DESIGNED and BUILT by GERRY SPIESS

MASTHEAD LIGHT

JIBS (2)
39 SQ FT EACH

MAINSAIL
44 SQ FT

WHISKER POLES
FOR TWIN JIBS

REEF POINTS

SEA HOOD

BOOM

SHOCK CORD
FOR JIB

HATCH COVER
(Slides Aft to Close)

COCKPIT

HATCH BOARDS
(Demountable)

Yankee Girl

OUTBOARD
4 HP/Two cycle

SKEG

MUSHROOM VENT

PORTLIGHT

BALANCED RUDDER
(Tiller Extends Inside of Cockpit)

Art/ Martin Bree

1

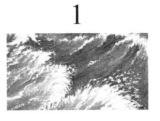

Overboard

Ten-foot Yankee Girl *and Gerry Spiess*
face a North Atlantic storm

Gerry's Story

SLOWLY, THE STORM WAS DYING. Though the waves were still racing at speeds of up to twenty knots, they were now only six to ten feet high and no longer breaking. After days of shrieking and howling around us, the wind had dropped to a more tolerable twenty knots—and, perversely, swung around to the northwest.

Yankee Girl bobbed downwind with the gray-green rollers. We were moving—an inch at a time—but moving, nevertheless.

It was June 15, the fifteenth day of my voyage.

Seven days of a storm on the North Atlantic had left me both mentally and physically drained. I was tired, dirty, and miserable.

I peered out a portlight. This morning, an eerie white haze hung in the air, and the sun was a luminous slit on the horizon. Big rolling waves heaved and boiled along the ocean's surface.

Enough! With growing impatience, I threw open the hatch, stuck out my head, and took a deep breath. Fresh salt air filled my lungs. It felt wonderful to escape from the stuffy wet cabin.

But when I tried to stand, I could not straighten up. Pain shot through me—my muscles and tendons had been cramped and squeezed for so long that they wouldn't function. All I could do was kneel with my upper body sticking out of the hatchway and my arms braced on the rails. Gradually and painfully, I straightened my back and held my body erect at last.

As I looked over the foredeck, I was relieved to see that the sails had withstood the breaking waves and clawing winds. The two jibs lay furled and strapped under shock cords on the bow, hanked to the forestays with brass snaps. The mainsail, held tightly with a shock cord against the boom, survived intact.

Though the speed and height of the waves intimidated me, I felt that the wind would allow *Yankee Girl* to carry a little canvas.

She'd welcome forward motion

I knew I would. It was time to at least try. My dream was still alive to sail to England.

I hadn't planned to design a smaller boat than anyone else's. All I cared about was building a compact, manageable vessel that could survive a journey across the treacherous North Atlantic, from the United States to England. That turned out to be ten feet long.

I had to keep costs down. I used whatever materials I could find that would work but were not expensive. I lucked out: One day, the neighborhood kids told me about a hardware store going out of business. Sure enough, we found plywood sheets in various sizes that had been used as shelves and partitions. I got the whole lot for twenty dollars.

I faced many design complications. I found that a ten-foot boat couldn't carry ballast: there wasn't room. Yet the ballast weight was what would pull my sailboat upright again if a high wave pushed her over on one side.

Gerry Spiess loved to design and build wooden boats.

Photo / Marlin Bree

"Gerry, old buddy," I said to myself, "maybe you'd better stick to teaching."

I mulled the problem over and finally thought that I would solve my problems by packing my gear and provisions down low in the hull. This weight would be my boat's ballast and give her the stability she needed.

Now I was finding out if my plan worked.

Yankee Girl's tiny bow didn't have much buoyancy; she would bury her nose in the water when I stood on the foredeck. My feet and ankles would get submerged—I would have to be careful of my footing. And work fast.

At the bow, I'd unhook the jib snap and pull out the jib from the deck shock cords. Then I would haul on the halyard to raise the jib. I had a break today: the small forward sail was already reefed.

Cautiously, I climbed out of the hatchway, clambered on deck, and grabbed the stainless-steel shroud with one hand and the mast with the other. Finally, I stood upright on the pitching cabin top.

I took a moment.

For seven interminable days, I could not see beyond *Yankee Girl's* immediate vicinity, and most of that was through the portlights. Now I relished the sweeping view and the open air. It was like coming out of solitary confinement. I could breathe again.

"It's a little like being on a trampoline during an earthquake, isn't it?"

A droll voice sounded in my head. I smiled: It was my imaginary friend who jumped in from time to time to keep me company.

"Too bad there's nothing to see but waves, Ger."

"When I tire of them, I'll let you know." I always had the last word.

I spread my feet apart on the hatch cover, thankful for the security of my safety harness and its three-eighths-inch thick dacron lifeline.

My plan was to time the waves and move forward between crests to raise the jib. With every muscle tensed and ready to go, I waited for the right moment—a lull between the waves.

But over my shoulder, I heard a noise. I turned to see a massive wall of water roar toward us. A new northwest wave—a rogue—had crossed over the old wave systems, flattening the waves under its power.

Mesmerized, I couldn't move. I hung on to the rigging and stared.

Suddenly, I realized that the hatch was still open. I had forgotten to close it when I'd climbed out. Now the wave was towering over it, threatening to fill the cabin.

Frantically I leaned forward with all my weight, hoping to lever the stern up.

The wave slammed into the transom, lifted the stern, and threw us sideways. I was plunged into the churning water as I clung to the shroud.

We were capsizing.

Gasping for breath, I watched as the deck went completely under on the port side. The wave curled menacingly toward the open hatch.

Yankee Girl was now so far down that I could see inside her cabin. If she went over any further or was stuck by another wave, she could capsize all the way. Then my safety line could wrap itself around her and I would be trapped below the surface.

Desperately, I kicked and struggled to get back to my boat.

What could I do?

Suddenly, I felt my lifeline snap tight. *Yankee Girl* surged upright—and pulled me up with her.

Her "ballast" had worked perfectly.

Everything happened so quickly that I'd been in the sea for what seemed like only a few seconds. Luckily, I hadn't even lost my eyeglasses.

With water pouring out of my foul-weather gear, I scrambled below and slammed the hatch shut behind me.

I slumped on my berth, thoroughly shaken and furious with myself.

Again and again, I pounded my fist into the soggy seat cushion. I had been stupid—standing up on top of the cabin, taking the time to gaze at the endless horizon. It almost cost me my life.

I became aware of my soggy clothing—and my pain. My raw, infected skin, which had been irritated by its unexpected saltwater bath, burned as if it were on fire.

The tiny cabin was partly full of seawater. As waves rolled us about, the salt rubbed into my wounds.

I splashed forward until I found what I was looking for in the bilge: a sealed canister with a clean shirt and a pair of soft cotton work pants. Stripping off my wet clothing, I patted myself with a towel, courtesy of another canister, and dusted talcum powder over my inflamed skin.

I felt better, but I noticed how my pants hung loosely around my waist. After fifteen days at sea, I must have lost at least ten pounds.

There was no way I could wash or dry my old clothes, so I threw them overboard, knowing that they would eventually disintegrate. I felt better after I'd dried myself off and changed my clothes.

I began cleaning water out of the bilge using my plastic kitchen meat baster and a sponge. The work went slowly.

I vowed I wouldn't go above until the next morning when it would be calmer. Besides, I needed time to center myself and think over the blunders I had made.

And learn from them. Outside, the weather steadily improved.

Morning dawned breezy but sunny. Overnight, the wind had swung to the north-northeast—perfect for a beam reach to the east. Best of all, the waves had settled down to only four or five feet in height. They seemed like ripples on a pond.

Crawling out of my hatch, I picked my way to the bow and finally hoisted the reefed jib. Then I hoisted the main. As I hauled in the sheets, I drew in *Yankee Girl's* sails to the taut curves that would power her effortlessly day and night.

With an exhilarating surge, *Yankee Girl* began to slice through the water. We were sailing a course for England for the first time in eight days.

"Looks like your luck is changing, Ger," my imaginary friend broke in.

"We'll make it yet, old buddy," I replied.

I was feeling cheerful. Earlier, that might have made me incautious, but now I knew better. Even though it would have been delightful to sail with the hatch open, I kept it closed to seal out the spray.

Everything was going so well I let *Yankee Girl* fend for herself. My self-steering setup with rubber tubing was nothing fancy or electronic. I brought the starboard jib sheet into the cabin, passed it through a block, and pulled the end back to the tiller. Two pieces of surgical tubing—like giant rubber bands—connected the tiller from the opposite side. The resulting tension gave us our self-steering.

This arrangement allowed *Yankee Girl* to continue moving on her present course, but relative to the wind. I had a pleasant surprise, for she sailed straighter and faster than if I were steering her.

One disadvantage to my self-steering setup was that it took up a lot of space inside the cabin. Because of the lines to the tiller, I could no longer sit in my favorite place: with my back against the transom.

Nor could I use my tiller seat because that would interfere with the lines. I couldn't even stick my feet inside the footwell. It overflowed with my supplies and gear, including forty issues of *Readers Digest,* a pair of shoes, spare lumber, a bucket, and some grapefruit.

I soon found that I was most comfortable stretched across the cabin in a semi-reclining position. I couldn't see the water, but I enjoyed the sound of the waves—and the miles—rushing past.

Even on an empty ocean, I forced myself to do quick lookouts. I'd rise, slide back the hatch, and scour the horizon for ships. I didn't expect any, but it didn't hurt to check.

Nothing was out there but waves. I closed the hatch.

If and when the seas calmed down to the point where I could leave the hatch open, I'd have a long list of chores to tackle. For the moment, there was nothing for me to do but lie back, relax, and let my boat steer herself.

I was intrigued by my simple arrangement of blocks, lines, and tubing, and I spent hours staring at it, trying to figure out how it managed to steer the boat more efficiently than I could.

I also took pleasure in watching my compass display my little yacht's progress through the water. We were heading east, or 110 degrees magnetic.

Whenever *Yankee Girl* hit a wave, the needle would veer over toward 120 degrees, slide back up to 100 degrees, and finally settle on 110 again.

Under sail and steering herself, *Yankee Girl* zipped along for three days and three nights at near hull speed.

Slowly, we both recuperated from the storm. My boat and I had come through with amazingly few losses: the gas cans I'd strapped on deck and the sea anchor. There had been a cracking noise down below, but I'd never been able to locate it; eventually, I stopped worrying about it. *Yankee Girl* seemed structurally sound, and there was no new seawater in the bilges.

Sometimes, I listened to the radio. The Canadian Broadcasting Corporation's programs were my favorites. They'd be in English in the mornings, but they'd alternate between French and Cree or Angokok—Indian and Inuk dialects—later in the day. Even though I did not under-stand what the afternoon announcers were saying, I liked the company of their friendly voices.

I began forcing myself to eat regularly. The weather was good, and the sailing was easy, but I had no guarantee that these conditions would last.

I couldn't afford to lose any more weight or strength. My appetite had improved, too.

I'd relied on my rough calculations to figure out my position while *Yankee Girl* was gyrating through the waves. On the nineteenth day of my voyage, I took some sights: I had covered one-fourth of the distance to England—over eight hundred and twenty-five nautical miles. I was delighted—until I realized that I'd been traveling only forty-three miles per day. I was still behind schedule.

I longed for a day of calm. I had a great deal to do, and I felt frustrated by the waves preventing me from completing my work.

I wanted to check my motor, which had been hit hard in the storm. It hung unprotected from its outboard bracket on the transom, and waves hit it so hard I thought they would tear it off. Though I'd pulled the starting cord through several times, it hadn't even coughed. I pondered if it would ever start again.

I was also eager to nail down the nylon transom flap that had let in so much water during the storm. And I needed to get the food out of the forward compartments and inspect the bilges.

My navigational fix showed I had sailed 1,200 miles by the twenty-third day. England, at last, seemed a reality. I had only 2,500 miles to go.

The Gulf Stream was carrying us northward, closer to the shipping lanes. We would soon enter an area of heavy traffic, that part of the North Atlantic in which ships "turned the corner" to avoid icebergs coming down from the north.

Soon, we'd be within the iceberg limit, but I didn't expect to see any of these floating mountains. Nor did I want to.

I wanted to stay south of the shipping lanes, away from the possibility of collision. I hadn't seen a ship for two weeks, but the weeks at sea had made me tense and edgy. Little things were getting on my nerves. One day, I was fumbling for a piece of candy when I bumped the button on my foghorn. The loud *b-l-a-a-t* made me jump.

"That was funny," my friend chuckled. "Do it again."

I wasn't getting more than an hour of uninterrupted sleep at a time. Often, I'd just be dropping off when a midnight squall would rouse me out of my bunk. I'd get up and douse the sails. I still hadn't found a genuinely comfortable position inside the cramped cabin.

My fatigue was beginning to show, and I knew it. I was becoming careless again.

One morning, I decided to have a breakfast of granola for the first time during my voyage As I bent over the stern to wash my red plastic bowl, I dropped it. I knelt there, helplessly, and watched it float away. I might have been able to turn around, go back and retrieve it, but I was too tired.

We were now making good progress, averaging sixty nautical miles a day. Though I kept the hatch closed because of spray—and that would not stop until the waves subsided—I was able to leave the drop board out and get fresh air.

I'd watch the compass for hours at a time, mesmerized by its deliberate, predictable movements. Now we'd be at 80 degrees, then 90, and we'd hit a wave and slip back to 80. Or we'd be at 90, then 100, and we'd heel and return to 90 again.

One hundred degrees was as far as we could go to the east. Since the magnetic variation was running at about twenty degrees west, we needed to sail 110 degrees by the compass to go east. But the little bit of northing we were making wasn't hurting that much.

I was primarily concerned with staying south of the shipping lanes, away from the possibility of collision. Occasionally, I'd scan the horizon for ships, just in case.

I hadn't seen a ship for nearly two weeks. It seemed like I had the Atlantic all to myself. I was growing accustomed to being alone.

I fell into a routine. I'd eat my evening meal early, wash my pan and spoon, and gaze at the setting sun, relishing every hue and ray of light. Then, I'd slink into my little cavern of a cabin and slide the hatch shut.

Immediately after sunset, the air cooled, and the moisture the sun had drawn upward during the day suddenly descended in heavy condensation. I knew that if I left the hatch open, everything inside the cabin would be saturated within a few minutes. I missed watching the night fall over the ocean, but I always forced myself to close the hatch.

During the next hour, I usually listened to my tape recorder and sang along with Linda Ronstadt or the Powdermilk Biscuit Band. Somehow, the music had the power to waft me home, to carry me back to the pines and birches and sparkling blue water.

I spent many evenings lying curled up on my bunk, dreaming about my family and friends. I imagined that someone I loved appeared out of nowhere and greeted me with a kiss or put an arm around my shoulder, or just sat beside me and asked how I was.

Then, rocked by my boat's gentle motion, I'd fall asleep.

Tonight I awoke early and poked my head out of the hatch to look for ships. Nothing was out there. I lay down for another rest. I glanced at my watch: 9:30 p.m.

At 10:30 p.m., my inner alarm woke me again. I moved toward the hatch—and stopped. I hadn't seen a ship for days. The chances that I would now, at this very minute, were slim.

Why bother? Besides, I was hungry. I'd eat now—and check later.

I turned on my small battery-powered cabin light. In its dim glow, I rummaged through my provisions until I found a can of peaches.

The dull glow from my radio's dial would give me plenty of light to eat by. It seemed silly to waste battery power.

I turned off the cabin light. I sat back, relaxed, and started digging into the peaches in the near dark.

Blazing light suddenly flooded *Yankee Girl's* cabin, streaming in through her portholes. For one wild moment, I thought a spaceship had landed on top of us.

I heaved the hatch open and stared in disbelief. Only a hundred feet away, a towering wall of steel slid by. Engines rumbled, bow waves crashed.

A giant ship had barely missed us.

Blinded by the ship's lights reflected off the water in every direction, I could see nothing on her deck. Or bridge.

I dove for my radio. "WXQ 9864... WXQ 9864... This is the yacht *Yankee Girl* calling any ship in the area. This is the yacht *Yankee Girl* calling any ship in the area. Over."

The response boomed out.

"*Yankee Girl. Yankee Girl.* This is the *African Comet.* We were surprised to see your light."

What light? What were they talking about?

"Didn't you pick me up on your radar?"

"Negative on the radar. We saw your light and tried to miss you."

The realization hit me. The only light they could have seen was the tiny cabin light I'd turned on for a few moments—and turned off again. But that light saved me.

I was badly shaken. Another thought hit me.

What would have happened if I'd slept only five minutes more? ✺

2

The Lost Ships

Giants slumber deep beneath Superior

"SHE'S OUT THERE, YOU KNOW," Dave Nixon, the charter master of Port Superior, told me. "I flew over her, and you can see her on the bottom."

I knew she was huge—well over 300 feet.

"Bigger than a football field," Nixon said. "A northeaster got her."

He had found the *Pretoria,* one of the largest wooden boats ever built in the Great Lakes, beneath fifty-five feet of water northeast of Outer Island. The water was clear, and he had a good view from the air.

It all began September 1, 1905, when the *Pretoria* loaded a cargo of iron ore at the Allouez docks in Superior, Wisconsin. Despite storm warnings raised by the U.S. Weather Bureau, the Pretoria took a chance—and put to sea.

She had no engines but was towed by the 263-foot wooden steamer, *Venezuela.* Shipowners found that two boats, a steamer, and a schooner-barge, could carry phenomenal quantities of cargo.

A lookout at the bow, *Pretoria* searches for a way off the lake.

Art / Marlin Bree

By evening, the weather had changed. Both captains knew that this wouldn't be another fall storm but a true killer gale. Winds howled at over seventy miles per hour; high waves battered the boats.

The *Pretoria's* steering gear broke about thirty miles northeast of Outer Island. Captain Charles Smart signaled *Venezuela,* and the tow vessel tried to alter the *Pretoria's* course back into the shelter of the Apostle Islands.

But in the heavy waves, the towline stretched—and snapped. *Venezuela* attempted to come about, but she lost sight of the powerless schooner-barge in the rough seas and darkness. There was little she could do. To save herself, *Venezuela* had to get off the raging seas.

When the *Pretoria's* captain ordered sails raised on her 100-foot masts, the canvas blew apart in the high winds. She could not maneuver nor steer; the schooner-barge wallowed in the rough seas.

The northeaster shoved the *Pretoria* sideways across the lake at three to four miles an hour. Waves smashed into her bulwarks, slammed across her decks into the cabins, and pounded against her hatches. Battered by the northeaster's waves, the enormous wooden ship flexed, planking twisted, and seams leaked. Pumps tried to keep up but burned out. It was the fatal blow.

Captain Smart ordered the ship's anchors dropped. At 2:30 p.m., the anchors dug into the bottom, less than a mile from Outer Island.

She came to rest within view of the Outer Island Lighthouse, where lighthouse keeper John Irvine was on watch. He reported in his logbook: "A terrible gale blowing from the NE. The biggest sea I have ever seen since I have been at the station, which is eight years."

Under the storm's pounding, the *Pretoria* came apart. Waves slashed across her deck and tore off hatches. Waves ripped off sections of the decking.

Irvine saw a small boat leave at 4 p.m. Captain Smart and his nine-member crew rowed frenziedly for the surf-pounded shore. The lighthouse keeper hurried to the beach, waving a white flag and carrying a piece of rope to render "what assistance I could."

A wave caught the boat and threw the men ten feet into the air. The lighthouse keeper helped save the captain, mate, and seamen hanging onto their overturned boat when they washed ashore. Four seamen and a cook drowned.

The *Pretoria* settled on the bottom, her masts protruding above the raging seas.

The lighthouse keeper wrote: "I expect she will be a total wreck as her decks are all coming ashore."

The *Pretoria* was one of the world's finest and largest wooden cargo vessels—a wrecked colossus. Her bones attest to her size: 338.4 feet (LOD) with a 44-foot beam. Now she lies underwater, preserved by Superior's chill waters. Her ending marked the end of designing bigger and bigger wooden ships and the finale of the big wooden ship.

The lesson ultimately learned: wood flexes too much on big ships. Seams open up. Water spurts in. No longer would shipwrights try to construct such large wooden ships, even with steel reinforcements.

To survive, you had to go to steel plating for hulls. But sometimes, even that wasn't enough on Superior.

As *Persistence* rounded Point Detour and passed York Island, I could smell the pines and the greenery above the fresh-water scent of Superior. The voyage had been chill, with whitecaps, but now in the shelter of the Apostle Islands' northern-most island, the weather felt like summer again.

Sand Island reminded me that there is something special about an island. It is hard to define, but Sand Island seemed welcoming and inviting to a solo sailor.

Marlin Bree aboard *Persistence* exploring the islands.

When I tied up on a small dock, with *Persistence's* bow pointing away from land, I checked below our hull. The water was almost gin-clear down to a golden sand bottom.

Persistence hung on the air, tethered to the dock by a spiderweb of lines. I loved it.

To the island's northernmost tip was a lighthouse—and a legend I had to explore. I trod along a woodsy, overgrown trail until, at the edge of the sky and the sea, there it was, remote and forbidding. Sand Island lighthouse was built like a fortress, whose ramparts would keep out the inland sea and whose tower would shine a warning beacon to ships in fog, storms, and the black of night.

The octagonal-shaped light tower rose fifty-six feet, and I reached the light by climbing a steep iron ladder. Lake Superior breezes swirled by, chill and moist. The historic oil light flamed for the first time in September 1881 to keep its lonely vigil for ships out at sea.

I could get a good view of Sand Island Shoals, about a mile-and-a-half northeast of the lighthouse.

On September 1, 1905, a wild storm raged on Superior. The keeper Emanuel Lueck could barely make out a ship on the shoals in the oil lamp's feeble beam. That meant trouble. Despite its name, Sand Island Shoals was a ridge of solid sandstone.

The 372-foot steel-hulled *Sevona* had begun its voyage out of Superior's harbor on a pleasant night, with no wind but with heavy ground swells. The wind picked up and began to moan through the rigging. By midnight, it had grown into a full-force Superior gale—a dreaded northeaster.

Laden with 6,000 tons of iron ore and low in the water, *Sevona* began to take heavy seas on deck. It was time to find shelter.

Captain Donald Sutherland MacDonald headed the steamer toward the Apostle Islands. The islands would bear the brunt of the growing storm.

In the wheelhouse, the captain and the helmsman scanned the dark horizon for the Sand Island or Raspberry Island lighthouses. But through the sheets of rain and the spray of the waves, they could not find a guiding beacon. They were sailing blindly.

Suddenly, there was a crashing sound—and the impact of two more distinct groundings. They had struck Sand Island shoal. Waves pounded the helpless *Sevona* against the reef.

She broke in two.

The Apostle Islands

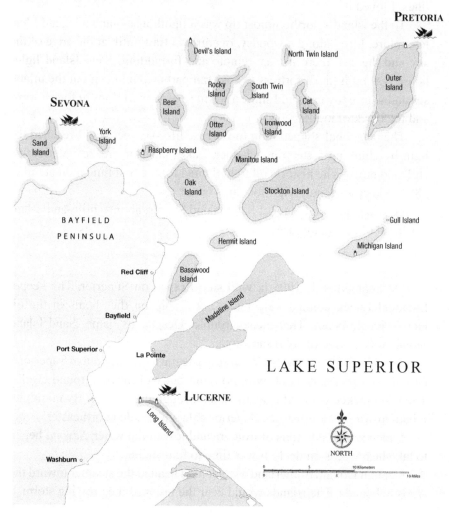

Map of the Apostle Islands showing the underwater wreck sites of the *Pretoria, Sevona,* and the *Lucerne.* (See page 19 for the story of the *Lucerne.*)

As light dawned over the raging lake, Captain MacDonald hauled out his megaphone to talk to the men on the aft section: Get ready to lower the lifeboats.

Seven men hastily constructed a raft from wooden hatch covers and doors in the bow section.

A mile-and-a-half away, the lighthouse keeper could only watch as twenty-five to thirty-five-foot-high waves roared over the *Sevona*.

The northeaster's waves pounded the lighthouse, with spray reaching as high as the beacon where the lighthouse keeper kept his vigil. He could not help the stricken ship; the *Sevona's* crew had to fend for themselves.

By 11 a.m., the lighthouse keeper saw that the crew had launched life-boats from the wrecked hull aft section. They pulled bravely on the oars, but one boat swept past the island in the waves and came aground on the Wisconsin mainland. The other lifeboat blew onto the island.

Captain MacDonald and his men dashed from the wheelhouse to launch their makeshift wooden raft over the side. Huge breakers inundated them in the icy waters, but they clung to the unstable raft and one another so that waves would not wash them overboard.

As the raft neared the island, the breakers grew larger. It bucked skyward—then broke up. The men disappeared beneath the waves.

Four days later, the lighthouse keeper found Captain MacDonald's battered body and other crewmembers along the Sand Island beach.

When I neared the Sand Island Shoals aboard *Persistence*, I took special care sailing from the Apostle Islands to the Duluth and Superior harbor. A cruising guidebook warned me to be wary of underwater obstructions in the shoals. The *Sevona's* bow lies a distance apart from the stern section.

She was still down there. I stayed clear. ❁

3

Raspberry

Life on a tiny lighthouse, circa 1920

MY CHARTS SHOWED that in approaching the dock, I needed to be wary of the western end of Marina Shoal, which reached out from the island. There were reefs, but as *Persistence* neared, we could see the rocks in the clear waters.

With my sailboat's shallow draft, we had no problems. I just pulled up the steel centerboard.

The Raspberry Island Lighthouse was once the showcase of the islands. Established in 1862, it guided shipping in the West Channel through the Apostle Islands to Bayfield. The City of Bayfield, Wisconsin, had been founded about six years before the lighthouse was built.

My wife, Loris, and I tied my boat on a long, wooden dock, then clambered up the steps to the lighthouse. We joined several other boaters who had anchored off the island for the night.

A man in an old-fashioned lighthouse keeper's uniform introduced himself as Toots. "You're in luck," he said, throwing out his chest. "I just took my Saturday night bath."

"You're not," the boaters responded. "We didn't."

Toots smiled. He was a seasonal park interpreter in the role of a 1920s lighthouse keeper and helped us re-create history. The effect sank in. We were in a time warp and had stepped off our boats to be transported back nearly a century. Bayfield was the epitome of civilization.

"You pay $1 a night for a room in Bayfield," he pointed out, faintly shocked at the high price. "Did you know that they have flush toilets?"

Despite these wonders, Toots was worried about trouble in the big city. "You look around on a Saturday night and see some young guys wearing mascara on their eyes." He shook his head at the misguided youth. "They've just seen a Rudolph Valentino movie and are trying to be like that movie star."

The lighthouse was a 20th-century fortress on the outside and spartanly furnished inside. Toots brought out a galvanized tub. "In Bayfield, they have indoor plumbing. But I've got this."

He looked about. "Do you want to try it out?

We shook our heads.

"Well, it just fits me," Toots settled his lanky frame into the small tub. His legs and upper body stuck out like a stork trying to settle in a kettle. He smiled, pleased with himself.

The lighthouse had other advanced features. "We collect rainwater off the roofs. We get our soft water that way."

On a table in the living room, a book caught my eye. It was a *World Almanac,* dated 1923. At night, Toots read by an oil lamp. A booklet on the table was open to an article headed, "President Harding's last public utterances regarding the flag, and the Star-Spangled Banner."

We walked upstairs into the emergency bedroom. Toots bent under the bed to pull out a little pot with a lid.

"What is it for?" No one answered.

"Imagine some night you have to go to the outhouse, but you see a bear lurking nearby. Well, you can just forget it."

He held up the pot again. Now its use became apparent.

Toots put a white glove on his hand. "Did you know that dust is illegal in lighthouses?"

He wiped his hand along the top sill of a door. "An inspector comes around with his white gloves; you can get fired if there is dust on his fingers."

Despite the strictness of lighthouse regulations, Toots loved his island life.

"It used to be after I got back from the Great War (World War I) that whenever I heard a car backfire, I would jump out of my skin. But it's so peaceful out here that I've forgotten all about that."

I felt sad as I walked down the long flight of steps to the water's edge and my awaiting sailboat. Thanks to Toots, I had visited another gentler time—one filled with joyful moments. It felt good.✹.

The three-masted schooner *Lucerne* lies loaded down to her lines as ice begins to sheet the harbor in this historical image. Floating high in the water behind her is an unladen three-master. Note the lengthy mast height.

Photo/Lake Superior Maritime Collections archives, UW-Superior. Superior, Wisconsin.

4

Ship of Death

At dawn, a dreadful sight

CAPTAIN GEORGE LLOYD HAD CONFIDENCE in his big schooner. He was a proud sailing man in the last era of magnificent sailing vessels— and perhaps he was resentful of the encroachment of steamships.

He declared he'd rather "go out with her under canvas than in the tow of any steamer." Under full sail, the three-masted schooner *Lucerne* dashed out of Ashland, Wisconsin, the evening of November 15, 1886.

As the centerboard schooner cleared Chequamegon Bay, Captain Lloyd didn't hesitate to drive his loaded vessel hard into the open waters of Lake Superior. She was carrying 1,256 tons of iron ore— 124 tons short of her usual summer load. It was a safety precaution for late-season weather.

The *Lucerne* was bound for Cleveland. Captain Lloyd intended to sail her across Superior to the head of the lake. At Sault Ste. Marie, she would join her tow, the steamer *Raleigh.*

Captain Lloyd's ship was one of the staunchest schooners on the lake with a reputation for being fast. Her dimensions rated her as a large schooner at 194.9 feet in length, 33.7 feet in beam, with 13.85 feet in depth of hold. She drew about 8 feet (centerboard up) and about 16 to 18 feet (with the centerboard down). Built in Tonawanda, New York, and launched April 23, 1873, the 727.9 gross ton schooner carried a cloud of canvas on three masts.

Fair weather lay ahead. Or so the captain thought.

But as dawn broke, the lake erupted in the worst northeaster in years. The *Lucerne* was heading eastward, up the rugged Upper Michigan coastline known as the Shipwreck Coast. The winds howled in her path, building enormous seas along a lee shore. It was the start of a blinding snowstorm that would sweep Superior for days.

Around 4 p.m., crew members on the steam barge *Fred Kelley* saw the big schooner off Ontonagon, Michigan. The *Lucerne* was taking a terrible pounding, with heavy rollers scouring her deck. All of her sails were up. She was beating hard against the headwinds and waves.

Captain Lloyd had to make a hard choice. She was giving him all she had, but it was not enough. With any luck, he'd return to the Apostle Islands and tuck in behind Long Island, about 60 miles away.

She was last seen turning about in heavy snow squalls and gale-force winds.

Three days later, on the frigid morning of November 19, the lighthouse keeper on the tip of Long Island woke up to a dreadful sight. From his tower, between storm gusts, he saw what appeared to be three ice-coated masts sticking out of the churning water.

As he fought his way along the beach to get a closer view, he detected what appeared to be ice-clad figures aloft. Three men had climbed the masts to escape their sinking vessel, lashed themselves in the rigging, and had frozen solid.

Men on *Lucerne's* icy masts.

Some were coated with six inches of ice. One seaman wore five overcoats besides heavy underwear, but his feet were bare. Another dressed heavily and had pulled on rubber boots. The third did not have much clothing but stood out in high-topped boots.

The ice-coated men in the rigging were all that remained of the *Lucerne's* nine-man crew.

When Superior calmed down, volunteers chopped out the bodies. They searched, but no one knew what happened to the rest of her crew.

There was speculation that some crewmembers were swept out into the raging lake after the vessel went aground. Others may have been entombed as she sank.

One decomposed body that washed up on shore about a year later was thought to be part of the ill-fated *Lucerne's* crew. They could not be sure.

The wreck marked the end of an exceptional ship in one of the worst schooner tragedies on Lake Superior. The *Marine Record* referred to her as "literally a ship of death" but could not explain her fate. It examined the tragedy:

> *"She was found one mile from the lighthouse... that she was lying stern on, with her stem in seventeen feet of water, heading to the southeast, showed that she had not foundered because she had cast anchor close to land and swung around in one of the most severe snowstorms that ever descended upon northwest lakes. She pounded to pieces there on the beach, and the terrible weather rendered the crew helpless. The continuous washing of the icy seas effectively prevented the men from getting ashore.*
>
> *"The sailors who took to the rigging tried to escape the season, but they only succeeded in running into the jaws of death in another shape than drowning. They were frozen to death."*

What happened during the big schooner's final hours? David J. Cooper, state underwater archeologist for the Historic Preservation Office, Wisconsin Historical Society, and his dive team spent many hours surveying, measuring, and photographing the wreck of the *Lucerne*.

"There's no doubt she met gale-force winds and heavy snow squalls," Cooper said, pointing out that she got as far up the Michigan coast as Ontonagon, where she was seen with sails set before she turned to run for shelter.

"It's also believed a pick-up crew manned her from Washburn, with boys eager for a sailing adventure. Though the *Lucerne* had been

The *Lucerne's* final hours probably came when a desperate crew member jammed a crowbar into the big schooner's windlass (shown on the right). An underwater archeologist records video imagery.

Photo/ Lake Superior Maritime Collections archives, UW-Superior. Superior, Wisconsin.

reinforced for her work, it was interesting to note, also, that this was her first season on Lake Superior."

It also was her last. Some observers said she was lost because she was under sail rather than under steamer tow. Cooper disagrees that sail power alone led to her tragedy. He noted that the *Lucerne* was designed and built rugged as a grain clipper for the lucrative Chicago-to-Buffalo run, a virtual grain clipper race. The first boat into port got the best cargo prices.

"It was possible that 'clipper fever' was still in Captain Lloyd, for he had served all his life under sail, and as a sailing master, he had a fierce pride in sail."

The *Lucerne's* wreck lies about two miles from the Chequamegon point entryway and about one-and one-third miles from the point light. She had been that near to the channel—and safety.

Captain Lloyd may have realized he was getting close, but he could not make out the light because of ice and snow. "Long Island is low, and he had to see it to make his entry," Cooper said. "He did not want to enter the channel blind, so it's possible he dropped anchor and tried to ride the storm out.

"You can imagine the conditions on board. Her canvas was frozen, seas boarded her with waves rolling down the decks, and everything was ice-coated. Her pumps and equipment were frozen—it was a terrible predicament."

In the *Lucerne's* cabin, divers searched the cabin's pot-bellied stoves, where they found the charred remnants of cabin furniture and portions of the cabin's sides. The crew used these for fuel after they burned up their coal supply.

Riding out the storm for two days, the *Lucerne* was taking a beating, open and exposed to the full fury of the northeaster. Her anchors dragged, or the capstan slipped, and the helpless *Lucerne* inched closer to the shore until her centerboard struck bottom.

One man raced up the mainmast, and two clambered up the mizzen. The way they were dressed, with one man wearing five overcoats but bare feet and another with boots but without warm clothing, suggests that the end must have come as a surprise. They must have grabbed whatever clothing they could and then dashed straightaway into the rigging.

But no bodies washed up on the beach. Cooper said, "Ice coated the forecastle and trapped the men inside; they could not make it out before the boat sank."

Down on the wreck, the divers came across a peculiar sight: an iron bar jammed in the windlass. The windlass is a winch-like device used to control the anchor's heavy weight—set it, or drag it up from the bottom.

"We did not know whether they had a problem dropping the anchor or trying to keep the windlass locked," Cooper said.

If ice coated the windlass, it would not let out the anchor. Or, it may have allowed the anchor rode to slip—and let the *Lucerne* move closer to shore.

He believes the crew was trying to drop the anchor. "Someone had tried to insert a crowbar to free it before the storm drove the Lucerne ashore—a desperate act."

Had she run ashore, bow first, she might have been saved, the *Marine Record* analyzed:

> *"… but when she let her anchors go in the storm, close inshore so that her stern wheeled around to the shore, her case was hopeless. Death to the crew was inevitable, except for a miracle, and the miracle did not come. It is probable that, in the blinding snowstorm, Captain Lloyd did not know that he was so close to land, or he would have taken the chance of driving her right on shore instead of letting her drag anchors in such a hurricane."*

The centerboard knifed into the bottom at about a thirty-degree angle. Cooper said, "That tells me they were moving backward, dragging anchor, and she struck bottom and broke her back."

The divers found a break in the keelson fore and aft of the centerboard. Those cracks were enough to sink her, taking her captain and all her crew to their deaths. ✸

5

The Long-Distance Cat

A near purrfect boat

IT WAS A SPIDERY-LOOKING CATAMARAN, low-slung and purpose-ful, floating in the shallow harbor on what looked like five or six feet of water. Down below her keels, I could see rocks glistening in the harbor's mud. The cat's light gray color was worn in places and weathered, and the twin-hulled windship appeared as if it had been somewhere and done something, maybe some long-distance travel.

I heard a whirring noise from shore and saw a man in an electric scooter gliding to the cat's starboard side. Lyle Burke hoisted himself into the cockpit. He did not use his legs, only his powerful arms.

"I've got the handholds memorized," he said with a smile. "Come aboard."

I stepped onto the gray cruising cat named *Sam* and moved into its low cockpit, topped with a permanent Bimini top. Lyle explained that he had multiple sclerosis (MS) and could not walk, except for scant distances with arm crutches.

He used his motorized, four-wheel electric scooter on land but swung about easily on the catamaran using handholds. Lyle was a remarkable sailor who accepted no handicaps. The skipper and his wife, Nancy, hailed from Duluth. Remarkably, they had just completed a 7,000-mile cruise.

Sam is an English-built Iroquois MNK2, a model with an extended stern, differentiating it from other Iroquois cats designed to be cruisers/ racers. Lyle's and Nancy's cat was 31½ feet with a width of 13½ feet. Built in 1978, *Sam* weighed about 6,800 pounds—a light boat.

When his MS deepened, Lyle faced a challenging time in a sailboat. He and Nancy used to sail a trimaran, but it was like a "skinny monohull," requiring lots of up and down clambering.

"My balance was not so good," he explained. The veteran Lake Superior sailors looked for a sailboat that would be easier for him to move about and be more stable. That meant a catamaran.

They narrowed their choices down to the Iroquois MK2 and found five to look at, with all but one boat in Florida. The MK2a, with the extended stern, was the cat they liked. Lyle added, "It was not a spur-of-the-moment decision."

Though low, the cockpit was large. Two wooden tillers extended forward from the transoms, linked by an aluminum bar. A single outboard engine hung between the two hulls, with controls leading to the cockpit. A sturdy, permanent Bimini top with handholds sheltered the cockpit.

Nancy and Lyle had the cat trucked from Florida to Duluth's Park Point, their home. Park Point is a long, narrow spit of sandy land that separates the Duluth/Superior harbor from Lake Superior and is the world's largest freshwater sandbar. They tested Sam in the harbor and then took her out on Superior.

Soon, Lyle and Nancy extended their cruises from several days to several weeks. They gained confidence in their boat and themselves and tried a six-week voyage. All went well.

They were ready for a longer—far longer—voyage.

In the fall of 1990, they had *Sam* trucked south from Duluth to Afton, Minnesota, where *Sam* splashed in the Saint Croix River. They hoisted their sails. It was the start of a year-long sailing odyssey that would carry them 7,000 miles.

They cruised downstream to the Mississippi River and then branched into the Ohio River. They followed the Tennessee River until they came onto the Tom Bigbee (Tenn-Tom) Waterway, which they followed through Mississippi and Alabama. Entering the Gulf of Mexico, they sailed eastward, "hopped along" the west coast of Florida, and enjoyed a sunny Christmas in Naples. They sailed to the Dry Tortugas and the Bahamas for about two months.

They broke a rudder. "It just snapped right off," Lyle said. Limping into a harbor on Eleuthera Island in the Bahamas, the cruising couple made a temporary repair, which held for a while. Lyle rationalized: "Monohulls cross the Stream on just one rudder. Why not us?" They crossed the Gulf Stream to Key Largo on one rudder.

At Key Largo, Lyle found a "palm tree carpenter" who "built us two new rudders in the shade of a palm tree." Sam's new rudders were constructed of two ¾-inch thick marine plywood sheets, epoxied into a solid inch-and-a-half thick rudder, which was then faired and covered with fiberglass.

They sailed up the East Coast with their new rudders, staying on the ocean until north of Miami. They entered the Intercoastal Waterway and found it "easy-going" until they came to Chesapeake Bay. They re-entered the Atlantic and, with trepidation, arrived at New York harbor. But they had their ride figured out.

"We caught the tide through New York," Lyle said. "We zoomed through Manhattan in about an hour."

Since leaving Minnesota, they unstepped the cat's mast for the first time to enter the Erie Canal. They motored to Oswego, New York, put their mast back up and crossed Lake Ontario, and, via Canada's Trent-Severn Waterway, ended up in Lake Huron's Georgian Bay. They entered the Sault locks and crossed Lake Superior to return to Duluth.

"The scariest thing on the entire trip was that once we nearly ran aground," Lyle said. The incident happened because they used an automatic helm, correcting their course with a hand-held remote control. They were relaxed.

As Lyle explained, he and Nancy are inveterate readers and "always have a book in our hands." Nancy looked up and asked, "Where are you going?" Lyle glanced up from his book.

They were heading for shore.

The catamaran brushed the bank, but Lyle steered away from shore in time. They found themselves with a souvenir. "We had grass stains," he mused.

He had forgotten to turn off the automatic pilot when they cruised beneath a bridge. The structure's magnetism had thrown off the auto-steering.

Storms on Superior? "We get used to them," Lyle explained. "The cat doesn't pitch; if we go into waves, the hulls pierce the seas and pop up. It's an abrupt movement, but they float up, as opposed to the yawing of a monohull. It's a dry ride."

"The more wind you get, the faster the cat wants to sail. What you do is reduce sail until you're comfortable. You point fairly well; downwind in Superior's waves is deceptively friendly. You run steadily and don't thrash side to side. A downwind run is like you're on railroad tracks."

"We've been in some rough stuff, but we're on autopilot. Once, we came into the Superior entryway with a northeaster blowing and high waves. Several big freighters were anchored off the entryway, waiting for the storm to subside. When our cat went down in a trough, and I stood in the cockpit, we were down deep enough to lose the 60-to-70-foot-high freighters from sight."

"We just rode the northeaster in. It was not a scary ride, but you must be careful under sail."

As experienced Superior sailors, Lyle and Nancy constantly watch for a weather front. "You can see it coming from the northwest," he said. "And you can feel the dead calm preceding it. Then you know it's time to head out of there."

"We pay a lot of attention to the weather. If it turns foggy, we turn around and go back to port. If it's not fun, why do it?"

I looked closer at their catamaran's outboard. It was a 10-horsepower, four-stroke long-shaft Yamaha outboard hanging off the transom and open to all storm waves. The little engine powered the Burkes on their 7,000-mile cruise when there was no wind.

Lyle showed me how easy it was to lower the engine's drive shaft via a swinging bracket into the water. Then he pushed a button, and an electric starter brought the two-cylinder engine to a healthy rasp. Remote controls let Lyle twist the throttle and shift gears. The Burkes cruised their cat under power at around five ¼ knots "for reasons of economy."

Lyle let me work the tiller bar, and I felt how pleasantly the cat steered. I was growing fond of this cat and its well-laid-out controls. It would be a pleasure to sail in all conditions.

A flash of something small and furry in the cabin caught my eye.

"That's Ming," Nancy said. "We have a ship's cat on board, and she is Siamese."

Ming cruises everywhere with the Burkes but has her own view of strangers. She disappeared when I went below with Nancy and Lyle.

Inside the streamlined cabin, the Iroquois had standing room near the cockpit but forward and to the sides, the area narrowed to somewhat less than full headroom. But it was wide and comfortable—and seaworthy.

As I seated myself, Ming came over to me. She was a beautiful three-year-old seal point. "We don't keep her below," Lyle explained. "She chooses to be below. If we are underway, she finds a comfortable place. When we dock, she comes out."

"Of course, she gets shore leave," Lyle said with a grin.

Everything had its place. There were bunks filled with gear, but I wondered where the small cat carried Lyle's electric scooter for his shore excursions.

"It comes apart in sections," Lyle explained. "The batteries and the rear drive go in the starboard stern compartment; the basket and cowling go in the spare bunk; the front unit and wheels are stored in a forward compartment. It takes about five minutes to disassemble." I admired Lyle's ingenuity.

"We've spent more time sailing since I was diagnosed with MS than before," he said. "We savor our time on the water a little more. I can't stand on the foredeck, for example, to anchor. I can't get off the boat to tie up. For that, I need crew." He nodded warmly toward Nancy. She was Lyle's crew.

Why was the boat named *Sam*? "It's after our deceased cat, Sam," Lyle explained. "He was with us for 15 years and was a unique cat. He died the year before we got this boat. We thought it would be great to have our new cat named after our last cat." ❄

6

Gold Fever

Gold! Cry echoes on Superior's North Shore

THE LAND AND SKY mesmerized me on the Queen's Highway. Mists swirled about as I drove along Superior's northern shores, crossing eastward around the enormous lake on the Canadian side.

I had some things to catch up on. A gold strike had been reported in a moose pasture. Rumors had spread that it was a big one, and I felt a little like a modern-day Jack London in search of goldfields.

I once had done some amateur "prospecting" when I was a boy. In the Cascade mountain range in Washington, my parents and I learned the art of panning for gold from an old prospector. He demonstrated how to use a blackened metal pan, put in gold-bearing gravel, and swirl it about in water until the gold drops to the bottom. He took us to a swift-moving mountain stream with moss attached to rocks. I'd wade out in the icy water, tear off some moss, put it in my pan, and swirl the stuff around. Eventually, we got a quarter of a test tube of the dark, sandy-looking stuff the old prospector said was gold-bearing. It was all fun, of course. But now, I was headed to where the real stuff lay underground.

It was not the first time Superior's minerals had caught the headlines. On this northern shore was a deserted underwater silver mine that was once the richest in the world. I spent a stormy night on Silver Isle's docks.

As I looked out my window, I could see clouds scraping against the pine-clad mountains of the Canadian Shield. On one side was sky: the other sloped downward to a rock-hewn shoreline and Superior's pounding surf. Round, rugged islets dotted the shoreline.

Spectacular as the scenery was, I felt isolated from the reality of the enormous lake. But that would change. I still had a sailboat passage to complete. That would be when my quest for the gold fields was over.

Fall was coming soon. I could feel it in the air.

Down a steep road to the waterfront, I began looking for an old railroad hotel. Soon, off to my right, I could see the Rossport Inn jutting up on top of an embankment beside a clear stream, not 50 feet from railroad tracks.

Built in 1884 as a railroad hotel and pay station by the Canadian Pacific Railroad, the Rossport Inn's rock foundation and rugged timber construction showed its lineage. It had been through much history in Superior's wild and remote side.

"When you're out on the lake around here and stop on one of the islands," innkeeper Ned Basher told me, "you feel you're Robinson Crusoe. If you found another footprint, you'd be surprised."

I didn't doubt him. Basher was an ex-jet jockey in the U.S. Airforce who had flown over the area and fallen in love with Rossport and the old inn. He bought the building, cleared out decades of accumulated dirt from the Canadian wilderness, sanded 100-year-old maple floors down to their original lightness, and brought the inn back to life.

Basher and I peered over the harbor and the nearby islands from the balcony. Below me, a carefully mowed patch of grass beside the railroad tracks caught my eye. It was a bright area of green among the wild grasses and flowers of this old fishing village, but not what I expected.

Basher explained: "The Canadian railroad system is quite accommodating. They drop off fishermen, canoeists, and campers at all points along the system and pick them up a week later by prior arrangement. The train goes through here twice a day—that patch of grass qualifies as our landing ramp."

I stayed overnight, but Superior's north shore wilderness lay ahead of me with its beckoning goldfields. I had a problem: I did not want to appear obvious. Or like a greenhorn.

"How do I find Hemlo?" I finally asked.

"The gold strike is just down the highway." Ned was on to me.

"I checked my map. Hemlo is not marked."

"As you go to Marathon, look on the left-hand side of the road, and you will see development. It might be difficult getting in, but there are some large structures."

I wondered what I would find. Perhaps the days of north country bard Robert Service lived again: Rawboned prospectors, gold pans, gold pokes bulging with dust. Dance halls, old saloons, gambling dens, dangerous dreams. Painted wimmin.

The innkeeper cautioned me. "Many people are interested in prospecting up here, so be careful."

"What do you mean?"

"You might hear some very imaginative stories."

He wore red suspenders and heavy boots—rubber, not the leather lace-up jack pine type favored by timber cruisers. He was tall and thin, gimlet-eyed, and dressed in dirty green wool trousers. Salmon-colored underwear peeked from his throat and the rolled-up sleeves of his checkered flannel shirt.

With his grizzled beard and scraggly gray hair, he had not seen the inside of a barbershop for some time. My keen journalistic eye judged he might be a veteran of the goldfields.

"Yah! I am geologist," he confirmed.

Perhaps it was the smoke-filled waterfront saloon; maybe it was the lateness of the hour. But he did not appear to be a geologist.

"You know vat iss dere?" His north woods eyes shifted cautiously around the bar room. "Gult."

"What?"

"Yah, iss troo!" His eyes gleamed. "Huntsful und huntsful…Gult!"

He studied the bar's patrons to assure himself no one had overheard. None had—or seemed to care, so he continued in a muffled voice. "Eye haf found zee lost gult mine."

I remembered the innkeeper's admonition. "How did you find the lost mine?"

"I sturdy zee satellite photography. Zen, I find zee mine."

"You found gold?"

"Yah." He sensed my reluctance. "I sent zee samples to zee government and mining companies." He treated himself to another sip of beer.

"What did they say?"

"Gult!"

"Right here?"

His eyebrows knitted together. I had overstepped a fine line. "Ach! I am not divulging."

I tried another tack: "OK, then; How big are the nuggets?"

"Beeg!" He held the palms of his hands open. "Huntsful und huntsful."

"Where are they now?

"Hidden."

"Does anybody know about your find? The mining companies that already surveyed this area, for example?"

"No!" he roared, shaking his head. "Und nobody iss going to know, if dey don't come up with zee money."

"What are you asking?"

"Maybe hundred million.

"That's a lot of money."

"Iss a lot of money, but iss a lot of dough aftervard, too."

"What'dya think you got there?"

"Beeg find. Beeger than South Africa, second to none."

"That's fantastic."

"Maybe first to none."

Dazzled, I walked into the dark night. Below me, the surf boomed. I had met my first prospector. I wondered what Jack London would have done.

Late the next day, I pulled into a roadside Canadian café. I tried to envision a gold rush, but as I drove the highway along the shoreline, I saw no prospecting or grizzled old prospectors panning for gold.

This wild area of the Canadian north shore seemed almost deserted. A lot of trees, though. Some rocks.

The small, dark-eyed waitress hustled over. Her name was Elna. She told me she had lived here all her life since this was a moose pasture.

"Didn't you know that there was gold here?" I inquired.

"No." She shrugged. "Did you?"

I thought for a moment. "What happened? Did somebody pan for gold, and one day, there it was?"

"No, nothing like that," Elna replied with a smile, leaning forward on the counter. "The mining company suspected there was gold, then checked into it—and so they just found the largest gold strike in North America."

"And now everybody's got gold fever."

"No one's feverish here," she said, wiping off the counter. "Not even lukewarm."

I pulled out my ace: a wrinkled newspaper clipping.

GOLD! CRY ARISES FROM SUPERIOR'S NORTH SHORE.

It was a headline in the *Minneapolis Star Tribune*. I had carried it with me on *Persistence*—taped to the cabin's nav station—and now to the goldfields.

"Estimates to be worth over five billion dollars…gold rush… prospecting fever spreads," the article went on.

"Here?" she sniffed. "You mean with the donkeys, and the pans, all over the countryside? She laughed. "No, no! Today it's all mechanized, with lots of technical people, lab work, and mining specialties.

"Mining today involves little specs in the ore. It takes tons and tons of ore to make an ounce of gold and loads of technology. It's not something you can just pick off the ground."

Perhaps disappointment showed more than I thought. Elna continued to enlighten me:

"Some friends went down into the mine. The mining company showed it to the townspeople."

I became alert—a report from deep inside a modern gold mine. "What did they find?"

"Black. It was pitch black down there. When they shined a light around, they just saw little bitty specs in the ore." She sensed my disappointment. "How about a refill on that coffee—and got any more good newspaper clippings?"

I drove some more until I wondered if I had missed the goldfields. Then, off to the north, I saw brightly colored structures that looked like part of a transplanted North Sea oil rig. Driving up to the Tech-Corona Mine,

I met Denis Lanteigne, a gold miner, before becoming a security guard.

What is it like down there?

"Down around twenty-six hundred feet," he told me, "it's cold, around freezing and damp. You see with a small light on your battery-powered cap. It's pitch black, and there's no other light source around; you feel you're blind. If you turn out your lamp and stand in the dark, you lose your balance and fall over."

The thought of going down twenty-six hundred feet rolled around in my mind. Was it worth it? "Can you pick nuggets out of the walls?"

"Here, it's in very minute traces. I've heard the percentage of gold per ton is from seventeen one-hundredths of an ounce to thirty-two one-hundredths per ton."

I wondered how they found gold in such microscopic quantities.

"They take core samples, like a slice of cheese, and analyze them. It's accurate: they know where the gold is, in what quantity, and how to get it. They can pretty well pinpoint the vein."

"How do you know where to dig?"

"They tell you to go straight where you're going, up or down, or turn left sixty degrees."

"But you can't tell. You can't even see the gold."

"It's too small. It doesn't reflect in the light, and you can't see it in the rock."

I shook my head in wonderment. "How rich is the Hemlo field?"

"One-third of the world's gold production."

"Where can I find some?" I was joking.

"You passed right by a large outcropping of gold-bearing rock."

"Right by the entryway?"

"That enormous pile of rocks."

I had a thought.

"Mind if I have a sample?"

"We got more than we need."

I selected a rock about 12 inches long and 8 inches wide at the pile of stones. I turned it over: it was a dull, dark gray color. Nothing glittered.

I carried it back to my boat and placed it in the bilge. Now my little sailboat had a souvenir of Superior's gold mines and a novel form of ballast.

Gult. I wonder what Jack London would have written. ✸

7

Isle Royale

Wolves, moose, lost mariners—and shipwrecks

WHITE FOG ENGULFED US. Through the misted windows of the ship's bridge, I could barely make out the bow of the steel vessel and a glimpse of Superior's cold, glassy waters. Visibility was poor, perhaps only 20 meters.

Wenonah was doing six knots, but time and distance seemed suspended by the fog. We floated halfway between water and air.

At the wheel, Capt. Stanley Sivertson squinted into the fog bank. The radar's concentric electronic rings spun out into nothingness, save at the far edge, where its beam outlined and held the island's mass for a few shining moments. Then it disappeared.

Isle Royale is a 210-square-mile island that is one of the last remaining unspoiled domains for wolves and moose. To me, it represented the Northwoods primeval.

Shipwrecks lay on the island's underwater reefs; ancient Indians had come here to mine copper so pure it had startled the world. A tiny Norwegian fishing village had once clung tenaciously to its tip, but that was gone. A few hardy campers ventured to the island; the National Park Service kept several rangers. But for the most part, Isle Royale was wilderness.

"We're in the channel," the captain announced.

The world was silver. I peered into the heavy fog, but I could see nothing.

"We've got to ease our way in," he said. "We need to get past a sunken wreck, *America,* and squeeze by the other channel. Maybe if you look out, you can see something."

I stuck my head out the window and felt mist on my face and glasses. But nothing else seemed to be out there.

"Up high."

Branches peeked out from the fog. The pine tree looked like it was right on top of us.

"That was close," I muttered as *Wenonah* glided through the rocky gorge. Capt. Sivertson smiled.

"We're entering Washington Harbor, bound for Windigo Station,"

We ran out of the fog bank and emerged into bright sunshine and blue skies. Summer had returned inside the Isle Royale harbor, and it felt odd to be warm again.

"We'll be here for several hours," Capt. Sivertson warned me as we docked. "So be back by the time we sail, or you'll have to spend the night on the island."

I stepped out on the wooden dock and looked about. Ahead lay a rustic ranger station. As I walked toward it, I noticed that my nights of sleeplessness were catching up with me. I was beginning to fall asleep, almost on my feet.

Then I remembered that wolves, an endangered species, inhabited this island. I hurried on.

"Threatened and endangered," Bruce Reid of the National Park Service confirmed. "Their largest concentration in the continental United States is on the north shore."

"Why study them on this island?"

"You fly the North Shore of Minnesota and see a wolf, and the wolf hears a plane, and he's gone," the ranger explained.

"But a flying researcher can circle a pack for twenty or thirty minutes after the island wolves hear him. As long as you don't get to a threshold altitude where it becomes an annoyance to the wolves, they'll go about their business. Here they've never been hunted or pursued; they don't have any experience dealing with man."

"Ever felt threatened?"

"Never even seen one. You can walk down any of the trails in this park, and you will see wolf tracks or their scat. They're here, but they avoid us as much as we would avoid them.

"Visitors and those of us here the bulk of the year rarely see a wolf, except in winter. I have yet even to hear the wolves howling, but maybe I sleep too sound. They have been heard here in the Windigo area this summer, but I guess I didn't wake up in time."

I began walking along the trail. There were no automobile roads or automobiles, only hiking trails. The " royal island" seemed almost unreal in its lush vegetation—like a Southsea Island paradise.

It was time to head back to the mainland. *Wenonah* cruised cheerfully in the sunlight toward the looming fog bank.

"Look closely at the water," Capt. Sivertson said.

We were in the channel, and the water was clear. I couldn't make out anything as I peered down into the depths. Then I saw a long, black shape emerging beneath the surface. We were heading toward it.

"That's *America,*" The captain said, turning his boat closer and slowing his engines.

Then I could make out her hull plates beneath the water.

Engines eased, and we lay alongside the dark hull. The captain began to tell me about this lost boat as if it had been a friend. Her end had come abruptly the morning of June 7, 1928.

As a boy, he had been on the island for summer fishing with his sister, brother, and uncle. His father and mother were coming over on *America;* he planned to meet them at the harbor.

"So we got up at one o'clock," he said, "but it was pitch dark when the boat came into the island dock. My dad was on crutches. We didn't know it then, but the doctor warned him not to go to Isle Royale. He figured my dad would not be able to get around on the dock or in and out of the rowboat we used to get to our cabin about a mile away. My dad looked at the gangplank—it was wet and steep—and decided he'd stay on the boat.

America was going up to Thunder Bay, then come around Isle Royale, and he'd be by at about six o'clock in the evening.

"Well, we went home and back to bed. We didn't know any more until we heard my father calling us, as if we were in a nightmare: "The *America* is sinking; the *America* is sinking."

"I ran out, and I saw my dad. Despite his broken hips and casts, he had somehow gotten into a lifeboat, rowed across a mile to our fishing place, and woke us up. I got into one boat, my uncle Chris and my brother Arthur got into another, and we went out to America. At first glance, we thought nothing was wrong.

The bow was right up against the reef, and when we got a quarter of a mile away, I said, 'It doesn't look like it's sinking to me; it's just sitting there.' Then I saw the boat roll over. I saw the skylights over the engines and all the windows in the passenger staterooms blow out like geysers, like fountains. Then she went down.

Capt. Sivertson looked deeper into the water. "I was so shocked at the sight of her sinking that this was the last thing I could ever remember of that night." He shook his head.

It was 3 a.m., June 7, 1928, and Captain Edward C. "Indian" Smith had an interminable day on the water. Steaming in moonlit darkness, the all-steel *America* had been on her route up and down Minnesota's North Shore, carrying passengers, freight, and mail from Duluth to Thunder Bay, Ontario. Wearily, Captain Smith turned the wheel to First Mate Wicks and a helmsman to keep the watch while he went below to rest.

Suddenly, *America* hit a reef with enough force to puncture its steel bottom. Capt. Smith rushed to the wheelhouse to command the helmsman to steer the sinking craft toward a gravel beach. He wanted to run the vessel's bow up on the shore to keep the boat from sinking until they could make repairs.

But *America* hit another reef, stopped, and started taking on more water than her pumps could handle. She came to rest about 30 yards off the beach. Hastily, the crew began to grease the engine to preserve it if the ship sank to the bottom.

The passengers were in lifeboats within an hour and on their way back to the dock. On their way in, they met several fishing boats coming to their rescue, alerted by the sound of their whistle.

America was beached like an enormous whale, with the bow run up on the reef and standing clear of the water while the stern hung down into the

Flags flying and passengers waving, the excursion vessel, *America,* steams out of the Duluth ship canal for a voyage to Isle Royale. The captain and first mate have the helm at the outside steering station atop the wheelhouse.

Photo / Lake Superior Maritime Collections, UW-Superior.

depths. The captain remained at his post as the ship sank, muttering that he would go down with his ship. But as the water closed around his ankles, he changed his mind and got off.

Capt. Sivertson concluded: "It had taken about an hour for her to go down, and the only casualty was a dog that belonged to a doctor. One of the doctor's kids wanted to go back, but the captain wouldn't let him. 'Don't go back to save that dog because your dad wants you more than he wants that dog.'"

The diesels of the *Wenonah* came to life, and Captain Sivertson eased his vessel past the wreck. I saw what remained of *America* fade in the black waters and finally disappear in the fog.

"What happened after that?"

The captain smiled: "Once the boat had settled and a diver had gone down and taken the safe off, we went out with long pipe poles to the front gangway to see if we couldn't find trunks and suitcases. We got some, but a neighbor had rigged a sixty-five-foot pole, and he snagged our family trunk. That was valuable, for my mother had all her keepsakes from Norway. So we got that back."

"But *America* was also carrying a big cargo of fresh fruit for Thunder Bay, Ontario, and all that fruit was in wooden crates. We fished for cases of oranges, cantaloupe, grapefruit, watermelons, strawberries, grapes, and bananas. We never had it so good.

"We'd make up pails full of lemonade; we'd have strawberry shortcake and banana cream pie. One island family had a little house just about full of bananas. The funny thing was, when you were on the wreck digging out fruit, once you freed one box, a whole lot more would pop up; they all floated. We thought we fished most of them out, but one night we got a real squall, and the next morning about twenty cases of fruit floated up along the shore by our dock, which was about a mile away. It was fantastic. All we had to do was walk down and pick out what we liked. The cold water kept it pretty well, too."

As a boy, Capt. Sivertson was part of the small community of Norwegians that lived in a fishing village.

"In the old days, we used twenty-foot-long wooden boats, covered only by a removable canvas spray shield, but otherwise open as they could be because you had hook lines going all over. The more open the boat was, the better. But that didn't make them seaworthy because if you had a big breaker, sometimes you could get them on board, and they could swamp you.

"The open boats were cold, too. I remembered one day I fished three hundred hooks, which is not a lot, but I was going up to the north side, and spray would come over. As I baited the hooks, I could actually see icicles forming on my fingernails. It was pretty cold fishing with bare hands."

"Ever think of another line of work?"

He shook his head. "I remember as a youth talking with this guy and saying, 'Oh boy, I'd like going out on the open water, taking on those seas with all those waves flying over the boat.' He told me, 'Wait until you get older, and you'll lose your zest for that.' He was partly right. Later, I gave up my open boat for a covered boat like those fish tugs they got around

Bayfield. But I missed the sun."

"Didn't anyone try to raise *America*?"

"They did. Some amateur divers bought the salvage rights to *America* for two hundred dollars, and one diver worked for a season to get her ready. When he returned the next season, someone had dynamited her bow and opened up her seams so that no one could get her afloat. Now she just lies there."

"Why would anyone do that?"

"It was done by people who wanted her where she lay. Now she's protected by the National Park Service as a historic site."

The old captain had seen a lot of Superior's storms, but he recalled the June 1964 storm he ran into after he'd bought the *Wenonah* in Chicago. He was sailing her home. As he entered Lake Superior from the Soo Locks, the wind was blowing from the southwest

One of the crew told him: "It's going to be a beautiful night on Superior."

"We got past Whitefish Point, and I started steering for Isle Royale at about 10 p.m. It was beautiful and calm, with no wind at all. I went down for a bit of sleep, but at about 2 a.m., I woke up wondering what was happening. The boat was jumping up and down and pounding hard.

"About daylight, all we could do was head straight into the northwesterly wind because we didn't want any breakers over the side or let them catch us on the quarter. We didn't want to take any more pounding than we were getting. When we idled down so we could just steer against the wind, I realized we were out in a bad one.

"I looked out and saw one gigantic wave coming at us, running above all the other breakers. In the sunlight, it was almost eerie; it was so bright. I wondered if we could go around it, but I realized I couldn't turn the boat: we'd catch the sea on the side, and that would give us an awful walloping.

"So we kept on going, and this wave would disappear behind other breakers for three or four minutes before it'd appear again.

"Then, it hit! There was a tremendous blow to the hull, and I held onto the wheel with all my strength. We were going downhill as though we had jumped off a cliff. We went down into this hole in the water that buried the bow and held us there."

The captain shook his head. "Then we came back up again, shaking off the water. When we got into Isle Royale that night, it became dead calm again. The seas had tamed themselves; the wind had gone down to a light zephyr."

We plunged ahead in the fog, and *Wenonah* glided over calmed seas, heading back to the harbor. I was walking along the rail when the first mate came alongside me. Something troubled him.

"My brother-in-law got killed out here in a storm one night. In his canoe."

"Why would anyone be out in stormy weather—in a canoe?"

"That's what I asked when my sister called me. I couldn't figure it out either. "I was living in Grand Marais, and I had gone to bed at about 10:30 p.m. when my sister called to say that her husband had gone out on the lake. All she could think of when I asked her why he went out was to answer: 'What do you think? The wind is up.'"

"She was in a state of shock. She said she'd called the Coast Guard, but they couldn't go out. I called some friends, but there wasn't much anyone could do if the Coast Guard wouldn't go out. We'd have to wait."

The next day, 15-foot waves on the lake splattered like spray guns when they hit the shore. A search party scoured up and down the beach for about eight miles in case the missing canoeist somehow made it back.

The Coast guard sent out a plane. At 2:30 in the afternoon, they found him.

"The way we figure it, his 16-foot aluminum canoe had been blown off the beach that night, and he went out to get it. He had been watching television and just slipped on his boots but didn't have winter liners, socks, or gloves. He took another canoe out, but the wind came over the treetops, howling down on the lake about 200 yards from shore.

"I figure something must have gone wrong when he transferred from the one canoe to his canoe. He lost the first canoe—we found that about eight miles down the beach four days later.

"When the searchers found him, he was right in the center of his canoe, huddled up. He was three miles south of his house and about

15 miles out on the lake.

"The Coast Guard said they couldn't understand how he could even be afloat because there were still 12-to-15-foot seas. But he had centered himself in his canoe and stayed afloat, despite wind and seas. There was nothing he could do. He had no paddles and no motor.

"That was how they found him. Still upright, but frozen solid in his canoe—and dead."

As *Wenonah* entered Grand Portage harbor, I peered into the clear water and saw reefs that were a lot closer to the onrushing keel than I wanted them to be. A wooden dock came into view; beyond that loomed the pointed wooden stockade of the historic seventeenth-century fur trading fort.

I watched the passengers disembark and walk down the gangplank. Soon only the Captain and I remained on board.

"Doesn't it get lonesome out here?" I looked out at the enveloping gray fog and pulled my parka closer.

"No," he said. "I have my diesels to look after."

I felt the lake's cool breath on my face.

The old captain shook his head. "This is my home. I don't leave."

8

The Diver

A professional copes with dangers

"ONE NOTION MANY PEOPLE have is that they will dive down and find some treasure ships. You hear this all the time. And they think they'll become a commercial diver and make a million dollars right off the bat, and everybody will want them, and there will always be clear water, and when they walk into a bar and say, 'I'm a commercial diver'—the ladies will jump all over them."

He had my attention.

I was in a diving shop in Thunder Bay, Ontario, amiably chatting with a commercial diver on Lake Superior. I noticed that he moved slowly and with a limp. He told me he had just been released from the hospital after a diving accident.

He sighed. "But in actuality, you build bumpers, swim underwater, take pictures and look at fish.

During my voyage on Superior, I visited waterfront dive shops to check equipment since I was a qualified SCUBA diver and to find out what was happening underwater locally. I was fortunate to meet local divers who usually had a story or two to tell, and there was much to share. Lake Superior is a treasure trove of history and underwater wrecked ships.

Divers were discovering sunken ships every season.

The diver continued: "When you become a commercial diver, you go into the water because something's wrong. Ninety percent of your work is in zero visibility and strong currents. It's cold, dangerous, and hard. You work your butt off."

"…and the ladies?"

"If you say you're a diver, they will run the other way."

Heh. Heh. No one had talked to me about diving like this.

I had questions: "If the water is dark where you dive, how do you see?"

"You don't. You do it by feel."

A typical diving job, he explained, is pipefitting. "You lay pipelines. Make joints, weld, and cut them." Divers also work with explosives and do photography. They also lay in concrete forms and work with jackhammers.

"When I go to work," he said, "I put on my suit, helmet, and coveralls. I have a crescent wrench in one hand and a sledgehammer. They drape a cutting torch over my shoulder." His diving helmet weighed 35 pounds, and his weight belt was 70 pounds.

"Why not use SCUBA?"

"The tanks have limited air supply. If you get caught on the bottom, you're in trouble. Another problem with SCUBA gear is that the regulator requires more effort to use than a hard hat. If you're working hard and sucking on that regulator, SCUBA drains more energy out of you than when you just turn the air on in the hard hat, and you have an atmosphere of air around your head. The pressure is easier to breathe. With SCUBA, you have to force every inhale and every exhale. And even though it's minor, after two hours on the bottom, it can tire you out."

I wondered about bottom time. "The longest dive I've spent around here has been three and a half hours. The typical dive is around 30 to 50 feet in the Great Lakes. At 50 feet, you can stay quite a while; at 30 feet, you can stay as long as you want. I've done a few dives to 140 or 150 feet; these come about once or twice a year. We don't have any reason for deeper dives."

He grew reflective: "Lake Superior can be beautiful and serene. Minutes later, you just know you're looking at death. That's why you find it challenging.

"Never relax on that lake," he warned. I believed him. ⚓

9

Storm Sailor

Rufus does it his way

THE OLD COMMODORE and I picked our way down a rutty trail amid thick pine woods. We had to leave the car behind us. The island path had turned impassible—ahead lay bogs of water and fallen tree branches.

"He keeps it this way on purpose," Bill Peet snorted. "He can get in, but few other people will try."

We were on our way to see the legendary sailor of Madeline Island, Rufus C. Jefferson. I had been on the island for several days and had *Persistence* tucked into the Old Commodore's slip in the Madeline Island marina.

"Is that his actual name, Rufus?"

"Oh, yes. "His daddy was a captain and quite a joker. And don't be surprised by his boat. He designs and builds his own. It's how he believes a Lake Superior boat should be."

"A friend of mine, the Red Baron, says he sees Rufus in a rowboat out on Superior, just watching his model boats sail."

"That's right. Rufus loves to build and test model boats of his own design. That's how he arrived at his twenty-footer."

"That's the size of my boat."

"His is altogether different. It's about as cobby a boat as you'll ever see; it's rough as hell. Rufus doesn't believe in fancy. He only believes in strong. It is as massive a boat for its size as you can find."

"Sounds slow."

"Oh, no. Let me tell you about our first Madeline Island to Isle Royale race. Rufus wants nothing to do with being called a yachtsman, so he was not entered in our race. At least not officially. But there he was at the starting line. He claimed he was just going out 'cruising'—in the same direction that we were.

"Well, he didn't fool anybody. Just as the race neared Rock of Ages reef on Isle Royale, Rufus's little twenty-footer was one of the first boats. But Lake Superior got to be Lake Superior, and when we got back to Madeline, there was no sign of Rufus.

"I was worried, so I hired an airplane to look for him or the wreckage of his boat. My search extended far enough, so I found him on the other side of the lake. There he was, he and his tiny boat, just sailing along. And when I talked to him on the radio, he dared to claim he had finished cruising—and now he just wanted to do a little *real* sailing. I got mad."

I smiled. "What did you do?"

"We sent him the bill for the plane charter, but he never paid. Sometime later, he showed up with a model boat he had constructed."

"And…"

"We accepted. It was a beautiful boat."

"Maybe that was all he could pay."

"Not Rufus. He just doesn't believe in spending money."

"Are his boats cheaply built?"

"Oh, no. Rufus builds in the finest materials that will do the job, but he will look hard before spending a lot of money. His woods are local for his keel and ribs; for clenching nails, he imports some zinc-plated steel from the Orient."

I shook my head. I had silicone bronze and stainless steel screws and bolts for marine fasteners on my *Persistence*. Real boaty stuff—not zinc-plated steel. And expensive.

The Old Commodore continued: "But everything on that boat of his works. He's had that little boat for over twenty years and sailed it all around the lake. He doesn't keep it at a dock—just a mooring out in Superior, and he chains it to that. It's exposed to every storm that comes along.

"Tell me if it's true that he only goes sailing when it storms."

"True. You know, that's when it's the most fun."

"Even during a northeaster?"

"Yes. But you have to have rock-solid confidence in your boat. You have to feel that even if it rolls over twice, on the third roll, it will come upright."

"What does he do in a storm?"

"He claims he gets bored and 'heaves to,' so the boat can steer itself slowly. Then he goes below for a nap."

The Old Commodore smiled. "He must get a lot of sleep."

Rufus C. Jefferson looked like an ex-Navy man with his close-cropped steel gray hair and ramrod-stiff bearing. He had rolled his work shirt's sleeves over his elbows, exposing his massive arms—the mark of a wooden boatbuilder.

He was about to clench-nail a plank to a steamed oak frame, one nail per join—old-fashioned boatbuilding. The 28-foot wooden sailboat he designed and now was building by himself looked like a throwback to an 1880 heavy-displacement Pilot boat.

"How are the Hong Kong nails working out?" The Old Commodore spoke first.

Rufus stiffened almost imperceptively. "Just fine. I have galvanized fastenings on my twenty-footer, and they've held up okay."

"True enough."

I had to ask: "Have you looked at the newer construction techniques, such as epoxy-glued wood?"

"It's not natural for a boat. The old-timers knew how to build good boats, and I've had success with their proven techniques. Besides, epoxy costs too much."

"You know, my twenty-footer? I keep it chained to a mooring in the lake. Sometimes when I look out in a storm, all I can see is the mast sticking out."

I glanced out at his mooring near a rocky shore. His boat was exposed to every wave, especially during northeasters. "How do you come into your mooring during rough weather?"

"*Carefully,*" he said.

He added, "You get only one chance to grab your mooring as you come in."

He turned back to his new boat. "Let me do a couple of fastenings, and then we'll go in the house."

"Can I help?"

Picking up a hammer, I located its head on the steam-bent frame and braced myself for the impact. He hammered a clench nail through the oak frame and into the Port Orford cedar plank in three noisy strokes. I could feel the force of the blows on the wood.

When the nail struck my hammer, the tip folded over. The single nail now clenched together the plank and frame—the old-fashioned way to fasten a traditional wooden boat. It looked strong. I liked it.

"Goes easy enough." Rufus was pleased. "And I don't use glues, either."

We walked up the hill into his island cabin. "No electricity, no telephone."

The living room was airy and filled with light from windows looking out at the lake. On the wood-planked walls were kerosene ships' lanterns, and a beautiful hand-carved church organ was in one corner. A ladder with a rope handrail led up to a second-floor loft. Everywhere, on display and in handmade boxes, were ship models.

"Good to have you back on the island," The Old Commodore said. "How long will you be here?"

"March."

I got it. Rufus was planning to spend the winter on this isolated island. He'd devote his time to boatbuilding. I envied him.

Rufus had returned from the Falkland Islands, where he helped survey the old clipper ships that had been there for eons. The Falklands are a graveyard for some of the last magnificent wind ships that plied the oceans. "I want to bring one of them back, if possible. They're part of our sailing heritage."

"But you have to see my boat now," Rufus said. "I have stored it all winter, but I'll bet my diesel will still start on the first pull-through."

His 20-foot boat was a double-ender, beamy in the extreme and full keel—like the old-fashioned sailboats. The Old Commodore was right: She was as cobby-looking a twenty-footer as I'd seen. She had a bowsprit and a wooden tabernacle

"Look, no fancy cockpit," Rufus said, swinging up and aboard. "Just big enough to stand in, and you can steer by leaning against the tiller." He placed the massive stub of a tiller against his back and moved the rudder with his body. "Nothing fancy, quite simple and strong. Nothing to fail."

"I've sailed this boat everywhere on Superior. It has never let me down. But let me suggest that if you sail alone, trail a line in the water. Twice, I fell overboard, and the only thing that saved me was that line. I grabbed it and pulled myself back on board. Otherwise, I would have watched my boat sail off without me."

"Now, look at this." He went below, and I heard him turning something over. With a cough of black smoke, his diesel engine came to life. "See? Everything works." He smiled happily.

He advised me: "You'll have a grand time sailing Superior. But be careful of northeasters, especially on the north shore. That's a dangerous place to be."

On our way back the wooded trail past the bogs of water, something occurred to me. "His diesel did just as he predicted. After being stored all winter, it started right up."

The Old Commodore raised an eyebrow. "He probably had it planned the way he usually does. My guess is that he took no chances—and started it in advance. When we came here, he knew it would start right up. And it did."❀

10

The Skiff

Behold the charms of an old-fashioned wooden rowing boat

THE QUIET WATERS of a shallow harbor stretched behind the rustic dock where I had tied *Persistence*. Reeds grew up through the water and danced in the light breeze as a mother duck and her ducklings paddled about. In the distance, pine hills marched down to the water's edge.

A painted sign on the pier advised they'd send a car if I wanted a ride to a saloon. I noticed a pay telephone nearby with the bar's number displayed. Another sign announced that overnight berthing was $5 and that I should deposit that amount in a small envelope (attached) and stick it in a pay box (also attached).

I had arrived in the laid-back Wisconsin harbor of Port Wing—my last stop on my voyage from the Apostle Islands to Duluth. I planned to berth here overnight, so I looked around. Near sand dunes, I found an outdoor pit toilet but no paper. There was no running water.

That alarmed me. I needed fresh water to make the all-important ingredient in a solo sailor's life—my morning latte.

I walked down a sandy road away from the dock, my plastic water jug in hand, until I saw somebody on a fishing boat.

"Where's the town?" I inquired politely.

"About a mile."

Towns along Superior's shores usually arranged themselves beside their harbors. Port Wing had taken a different tack: its village was on the mainland, hidden from its harbor. Port Wing had been a rough Scandinavian timbering town in the old days. I had been warned to watch myself in Port Wing because it could get wild.

"Down the road," he added. "If you need anything from town, I'll be happy to run you in."

Thanks. Just a little water for morning coffee."

"Well, if you need anything else, let me know."

I was surprised at his generous offer. I decided my brief stay at Port Wing would turn out OK.

I found a spigot down the road, filled my water jug, and began to trudge back. Near my dock, I slowed my pace. A silver-haired man in blue jeans, broad-shouldered and narrow-hipped, stood close to my boat, scrutinizing *Persistence*. I judged him to be in his sixties.

He would take a few steps, pause, bend closer to my boat, and then fall into a trance. Amused, I waited to see what else he was up to, but then he'd move a few paces and turn his head as if looking for just the right angle while scrutinizing the details.

I had found a fellow boatbuilder.

I was about to say something when he spoke first: "Nice job. And it took you a while, too."

"Seven years." I wondered how he knew I was the builder or knew I had walked up behind him. In my boat shoes, I had been quiet. "It's wood veneers coated with epoxy."

"That's not how I built them. But it's nice."

I took a step back. "You remind me of someone I just met on Madeline Island."

"Not Rufus Jefferson?"

"The same!"

His name was Bob Power, and he had lived on this waterfront for much of his life. He was a cousin of Rufus. They had boated everywhere on Superior in their youth—even rowing partway around the big lake.

"Rowing is a good way to travel if you have the right boat—a proper rowboat."

"I've read some sea stories where men have rowed across oceans. That always seemed incredible to me."

Bob smiled. "Let me show you something."

I followed him to an old boat shed by the water. As we entered, I smelled cedar wood tinged with mustiness. It was a good smell. I looked up: pulleys suspended several boats from the low shed roof. I could tell from the patina of dust on the hulls that they had not been disturbed in years. His varnished boat shone through the dust at the end of the row.

It was built the old way, with selected woods steamed and shaped into graceful curves to welcome the waters. From the tip of its pointed bow to the transom's wineglass shape, the boat had been designed for one purpose: to be rowed.

"It's beautiful." I ran my fingers along its curves.

"It's a White Bear Rowing Skiff. People, especially kids, always want to borrow it. But I keep it safe here."

"Looks like it was built just a few years ago."

"Nineteen fifty-seven. I built this boat from forms I got from a man who got them from his dad, who brought them over from Norway

I looked the little craft over. The planking was cedar. Very light. The steamed oak ribs were thin but strong. The stern looked challenging to build. Its underwater lines joined like a double-ended boat—but its transom swept out of the water.

"Why the wineglass stern?"

"The following seas pass right on by and don't hit the back of the boat to knock it off course. You look at old photographs of boats, and you'll see they all had the same double-ended idea. With the lift of the fantail, you can have following seas and get nothing over the transom. The boat picks up on a wave, and you'll just glide right down."

Nice. I let my eyes linger on this old rowing boat.

"Want to take her out?"

I hesitated. "I don't know much about rowing."

"You'll get onto it," he assured me as he untied a line. "But the boat has been stored dry for years, so the planks haven't swollen shut."

"How long will that take?"

"About twenty minutes. Maybe thirty. Then it'll stop."

The White Bear Rowing Skiff bobbed in the water as I stepped on board. Bob handed me the long, light oars.

I looked down. Water started to trickle into the bilge. "Sure it'll stop in twenty minutes?"

"That's about it, more or less," Bob reassured me with a friendly wave from shore. "Have a good time."

Alone on the water, I tried to get the feel of my first actual rowing boat. The small craft felt light in the water, and it would glide endlessly with just a gentle pull on the oars.

I tried putting a little heft into the oars. I moved smartly ahead. That felt good, so I did it again. This time, I missed a stroke—and promptly got a splash of water in the face.

I was soon among the rushes on the far side of the sleepy harbor. I rowed toward several ducks, which leisurely paddled out of my way. They did not take flight or even seem alarmed. A wooden rowboat did not threaten them.

Time passed as I worked on my technique. The exercise of seemingly effortless rowing was exhilarating. Everything was in motion—the boat, the water, and me.

I glanced down. Water was seeping in, just as Bob had predicted. Nothing to worry about. The planks would soon swell up, and the leaking would stop.

Sailors had rowed skiffs like this across oceans. It was handling beautifully in calm harbor waters—but I wondered how it would behave in waves.

I headed toward the breakwater.

Ahead lay the open waters of Superior. I concentrated on my rowing. I used my arms and shoulders, not my torso and back. I tried inserting the oars into the water and then leaning back.

It worked! We were moving faster with less effort.

As Superior's waves reached out, the boat sliced her bow into the onrushing water and began a graceful dance with the waves. We were a symphony of motion. Water gurgled softly against her wooden hull.

Suddenly, I felt cold water on my feet. I looked down: water was over the floorboards, sloshing back and forth. The water formed into a wave that washed my deck shoes when the boat bobbed.

Whoa! Had I gone too far—too soon? With a flailing of oars, I began a quick retreat to the concrete piers. Superior's waves seemed larger now.

I put my back into the oars. We seemed to be in a race between swamping and surviving. Chill waters lapped over my ankles.

Picnickers sitting atop a pier waved happily at me. One woman turned to her son: "Oh, look—a rower!"

I did not loosen my grip on the oars, but I managed a smile back.

At last, we were inside the protective canyon of the breakwaters—away from the waves.

Bob was patiently sitting cross-legged on the dock. "She swell up yet?"

"Starting to." I glided toward the dock. "At least the bottom planks don't seem to be taking on any more water."

"Told you so."

"Wonderful boat. I went out through the breakwaters onto Superior."

"You had a good row." He was pleased.

Bob held the boat as I got out, then sat down on the wooden pier. He tipped the rowing boat on its side with his bare feet, letting water swirl around the upper planks. They soon would swell up.

I sat with him for a while, talking about boats. The world seemed fine in the peaceful harbor, thanks to an old-fashioned wooden rowing boat. ❁

11

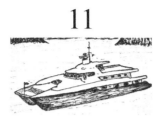

Hollywood Comes Calling

Can that be a movie star?

LATE IN THE AFTERNOON, as the sun cast surreal shadows over the waterfront, I noticed boaters gathering on the south side of the dock, pointing at something entering Rossport Harbor. Shading my eyes with my hand, I looked to the southwest. The craft looked huge even from a distance, with decks towering up from the waterline.

As the boat maneuvered out of Nipigon Bay and past Whiskey Island, heading for the channel between Quarry and Healy Islands, she presented her stern: she had two immense hulls. She was a giant catamaran, the likes of which I'd never seen on Superior—a floating palace.

The dock boy drifted by with a knowing look on his face.

"What?"

"Mel Gibson's boat," he announced. He caught my look. "Oh, it's confirmed. He's on board. He arrived by helicopter in Thunder Bay."

The catamaran slowed, and a white inflatable shoved off and roared toward us, loaded to the gunnels. Throttling back when it reached the inside of the dock, it headed for the loading ramp.

Two white-uniformed crewmen tied up, stepped off, and deposited dozens of large plastic bags near the dockside trash container. One crew member hiked off, importantly.

"Mel's boat?" Someone had to ask.

The Australian sailor aboard the inflatable looked up. "No," he said.

"But we've been having a lot of fun with that rumor since it started."

Not Mel, he assured us. "Nobody by that name aboard."

The crowd around me lost interest and ambled off. The sailor sat biding his time in the all-white inflatable in his crisp white crew uniform and white shoes.

After a while, the other crew member returned from his errand and clambered on board. They left in a flurry of high-speed spray.

By this time, the catamaran had edged its way up the channel between Quarry and Healey Islands and no longer was in sight. The inflatable pursued the big cat's wake.

I shrugged my shoulders, exchanging amused glances with one of the young sailors aboard a cruising boat that had just arrived at the dock. Someone asked, "Who'd thought he'd show up here?"

Indeed, who would imagine that Mel Gibson, multimillionaire Australian film actor, Hollywood director, and Oscar winner, would arrive in this tiny Canadian hamlet in this remote part of Lake Superior?

"Could be," the young sailor speculated, with an edge to her voice. "You know, he has a house along the North Shore, a spectacular one atop a hill."

"Eh?"

"Three things," she said, ticking them off. "One, the crew guy said only four people were on board, and I saw more than that with my binoculars, including children. Gibson has several children."

"Second?"

"The newspaper account was specific about the helicopter flight into Thunder Bay. A cop took someone out to look at the boat, which he identified as Gibson's."

"And third?"

"That runabout looked like it might take somebody ashore, but they got put off by the crowd. A movie star would act like that."

"You're good," I said.

She smiled a conspiratorial grin, pleased with herself. I edged away.

"He's coming in, you know." She leaned forward. "Under cover of darkness."

"What for?"

"To eat at the local inn." Excitement crept into her voice.

"The cat will come back?"

"Naw. A runabout. With Mel disguised as a crew member."

A thought crossed my mind as I began to return to my boat.

"You will keep a Mel watch?"

"Until dark."

It was irresistible fun. Here we were, a bunch of small-time boaters in this remote Canadian hamlet, sharing space with moose, bears, endless water, and woods, but now talking on a first-name basis about a Hollywood icon.

It was not Mel Gibson anymore. But "Mel."

The next day, I checked on the young woman who volunteered to do the Mel Watch. "Did he make it ashore?"

"Had drinks with him last night." Her eyes glittered. "Partied all night."

"And?"

"Oh, then he went back to his boat."

"To think I missed all the excitement."

"And the story of the decade. Some journalist."

"The world's loss."

To impress her with my sincerity, I threw in a deep sigh and my best Hemingwayesque grimace. She did not seem overly impressed.

All dockside chit-chat aside, it amused me to figure out what was happening. When the first officer of the catamaran had disappeared from the docks, he headed toward the Rossport Inn.

That would mean my old friend, Ned Basher. I trudged up the hill to the inn. Ned was not only the innkeeper but seemed to function as Rossport's official greeter, unofficial hamlet manager, and all-around Northwoods bon vivant.

You want answers; Ned had answers. The boat was *Moecca,* a 150-foot-long, jet-drive catamaran, a state-of-the-art luxury craft registered in the Isle of Mann under British registry. She had been built in Australia but flew the British, not the Australian flag.

"The Mel Gibson rumor started with us at the Saint Lawrence," the first officer had told Ned. "And stayed with us all the way here."

With an international crew of British, Greeks, Italians, and Australians, *Moecca* was cruising worldwide to entertain corporate executives and customers.

"You could charter her," Ned suggested. "A week on *Moecca* goes for $140,000, not including food, water, or beverages."

Yeah, sure. A boating journalist with a home-built 20-foot sailboat and eating food out of cans would not be a likely candidate to charter that luxury barge. But Ned knew that.

"Maybe not this season." We both chuckled.

I brought Ned up to date on what I had heard on the docks. One rumor was that the enormous cat was coming in for parts.

Ned liked that one. "I've got lots of parts in the basement. If they don't fit, we'll make them fit for Mel Gibson's boat."

A little more Northwoods humor.

"So, what did they come in for?"

"GPSs."

"Don't they have GPSs?"

"Oh, the boat has all sorts of electronics. But two guests on board did not have personal GPS units, and they felt lost. They wanted their own."

Moecca had been in radio contact with the Rossport Inn, and Ned had ordered the GPS units for the guests. *Moecca* came into port and dispatched the first officer and a crewman in the white inflatable to pick up the two hand-held GPS units.

And to drop off the trash.

After a few beers with Ned, I trudged down to *Persistence.* I was amused. Imagine detouring a giant catamaran for two GPS units.

I remembered the words of author F. Scott Fitzgerald: *The very rich... they are different from you and me.*

Not so amused with "Mel's boat" was the owner, operator, and chief fry cook of the Halcyon Haven, the tiny harbor-side shack that serviced boaters and fishermen.

"They came in with a runabout full of garbage bags and piled them up in front of the garbage bin. The haulers charge us $2 for every five bags."

"They didn't pay?"

"They sailed off in that big boat, and we're stuck with the bill."

She told me she received a telephone call from a Duluth newspaper reporter who had been following the progress of Mel's boat.

"And I told them."

"About Mel?"

"Naw." She drew herself up. "About the garbage they left. The reporter asked me if I had opened any of it and gone through it."

"Imagine going through garbage." She was indignant. "Or suggesting it. I told them: *No.*"

Her eyes took on a gleam. "But I told them we have to pay for picking up *their* garbage. Did you know the haulers charge us $2 for every five bags?" ✺

12

The Last of the *Sheila Yeates*

A voyage too far on the North Atlantic

IT WAS A FINE SUMMER MORNING. Monochromatic rays of light mixed sky and sea in shades of gray on Superior's broad waters. In front of me, bobbing in the harbor's waters, was the *Sheila Yeates,* bright with fresh paint and newly cut sails—a boat just beginning her life on these great waters.

Like traditional wooden vessels, her hull was built carvel style of wooden planks on oak frames. Her bowsprit jutted jauntily, and her two tall masts soared toward the heavens from her planked wooden deck.

Yeates had sailed across the Great Lakes from her boatbuilders in Lunenburg, Nova Scotia. She had been launched in 1976, just in time to participate in the Tall Ship ceremony in New York Harbor commemorating the nation's Bicentennial. Lake Superior was to be her home.

Her topsides gleamed in the morning sun, and I could see that this topsail ketch had character: her racy lines were patterned after a Civil War-era sailing ship. She was a beauty. At 50 feet on deck, with a bowsprit jutting out further, she was a sturdily built, ocean-going vessel that would have a wonderful life in this inland ocean.

I wished her well, this tall new ship on Superior.

Sheila Yeates was the dream of Geoffrey Pope. Planned in the 1960s, the vessel was named for the skipper's only daughter, Sheila, combined with his mother's name, whose maiden name was Yeates.

Captain Pope's crew members were people fascinated with the massive lake and wanted to learn the ways of an old-style wind ship. Volunteers spent spring weekends doing maintenance to refurbish and refit the vessel for each sailing season.

When the skipper taught a class in coastal navigation, I signed up. Captain Geoff Pope was a wiry man in his 70s. Despite his advanced years, he moved with the agility of a seaman. His arms were muscular and his shoulders broad—a true wind sailor.

Pope was an adventurer. In the 1930s, he canoed from New York City to Nome, Alaska.

"How many of you think it's a big deal to cross Superior?" he asked. Several class members raised their hands.

"Well, it's not. It's been crossed by all kinds of vessels, including even a few centerboard boats."

I smiled. My *Persistence* is a centerboarder, albeit a small one at 20 feet. She also called Superior home.

He recalled days when he and his crew took down sails in the middle of the lake to feast on lobster and drink chilled Chablis wine. It was a glowing portrait of life aboard his wind ship.

Though Pope was not one to take unnecessary chances, a siege of heavy weather didn't trouble him. When a storm lashed the open waters, a neophyte sailor boarded *Sheila Yeates* at a northern port. "I thought we'd stay tied up in the harbor, but we sailed right into the storm. Nothing seems to stop that boat."

He had grown accustomed to its moods.

"We were in rough weather, and I was at the helm," an amateur sailor related, "when a wave came on board. Two crew members ahead of me on the deck began swimming. I had to hold *Yeates* on course, but we were shoved around by that wave's grip.

"I was having a terrible time when I heard the skipper yell, 'Get back on course.'"

"Captain Pope had been down below, sleeping. He woke up when he felt his boat changing directions, however slight.

The *Sheila Yeates*

Another time, someone asked my advice. "I've heard stories about that lake. I wondered if I really ought to go out on *Yeates*."

I did not hesitate. "She lives on that lake. Take the cruise. You'll have a grand time." And he did.

More people crewed the green-hulled *Yeates*. I knew teachers and journalists who helped pay for her upkeep, taking time to cruise her for a few days each summer. They also held fundraisers for Yeates. I contributed a few of my boating books to be auctioned off.

As *Yeates* aged, her skipper seemed smitten with wanderlust. She dashed about Superior, crossing from the U.S. to and fro from Canadian ports, and explored little-known islands and coves on the rugged Canadian north shore.

In 1985, Captain Pope sailed across the Great Lakes into the North Atlantic to Greenland.

It only whetted the captain's taste for what was to come.

One year, she left Superior to wend her way through the Great Lakes, up the St. Lawrence River, and then dash out into the North Atlantic. Another 40 crew members would join Yeates at various harbors on the trip.

But luck wasn't with her on this trip.

She reached St. Anthony, Newfoundland, bound for Iceland, where more crew members were scheduled to come on board. But as she approached the southernmost tip of Greenland, she found herself surrounded by pack ice. And fog.

The ice was further south than usual. Massive chunks began engulfing the wooden vessel. At 2 am., *Yeates* went on the air.

"Mayday, Mayday."

Two fishing vessels tried to reach her, but the ice pack was everywhere. They turned back.

Kiviuq, a Danish trawler, heard her call and made her way through heavy fog, listening on the radio for the stricken vessel's coordinates.

Both crews shouted joy as *Kiviuq* broke through the ice surrounding *Yeates*. The Danish captain got a line to the stricken sailing vessel and hauled its crew on board the larger boat.

They towed *Yeates* back through the ice channel *Kiviuq* had already cut and exited the ice. Their course was easterly across the North Atlantic, toward Scotland.

Captain Pope radioed friends and crew members that he would have his wooden ship seaworthy in about a month after she reached port

Then she would resume her cruise.

Under tow, the wind ship rode well for about 400 miles until heavy weather hit. The Danish vessel's usual speed was 23 knots, but it slowed to 16, the least it could do, and still keep on schedule. *Yeates'* hull speed was only 6 to 8 knots. Even at reduced speed, *Yeates* took a pounding.

Storm seas began boarding Yeates, but Pope or his crew could do nothing. With the vessels lurching about in heavy waves, there was no way to keep an emergency crew on the wooden vessel. She had to tag behind, alone and unmanned—or be left behind.

When they stopped to examine her, she seemed OK. There was no water in the bilge.

Another storm hit *Yeates.* Wave after wave battered her. She rode lower in the water.

They stopped to check her over a third time, but now seawater rolled in the bilge. Had some of her seams loosened, or had a plank come undone?

They couldn't find the leak. No one knew what the problem was. Worse, there was nothing anyone could do.

She could not keep up. She could not be repaired or pumped out. With a heart-wrenching finality, Captain Pope came to the only conclusion he could: His beloved wooden boat had to be cut free.

It did not take long.

She grew heavy by the bow. Waves covered her bowsprit, and she sank into the water. Her bow ripped off. Lofting her stern to the skies, she slipped beneath the North Atlantic to rest forever.

The *Yeates* was 13 years old.

Captain Pope was desolate."It's the end of the line for *Sheila Yeates,*" he told reporters. "At my age, I don't think I'll be able to find the money to build another boat."

Several years later, I met up again with Captain Pope. He seemed almost timeless at age 80, with his white hair and beard. Topsail ketches were still the great love of his life. He had hoped to build a ship to replace *Yeates* at one time. But the cost of a new boat would be close to $800,000.

"What do you do when you don't have that much?"

He shook his head.

He had just returned from an attempt to navigate the Northwest Passage, a 3,000-mile journey from northern Greenland westward to the Bering Straits between Alaska and Siberia—an icy passage that killed sailors.

Pope had signed on as a crew member on the 57-foot fiberglass Bowman ketch, *Cloud Nine,* skippered by Roger Swanson. *Cloud Nine* had sailed up from St. Thomas in the U.S. Virgin Islands and had pushed 2,000 miles into the passage before ice forced them back. They turned around and ended their voyage five months and 8,000 miles later—in Falmouth, England.

Onboard *Cloud Nine,* Captain Pope had rounded Cape Horn, sailed in the ice of the top of the world, and circumnavigated the globe.

His beloved ship was gone. But the old captain kept sailing.※

13

Getting Wet

The underwater world beckons with a fickle finger

IT WAS LOCATED about 10 miles from the city limits of Duluth on a rocky promontory jutting out from the North Shore. The boathouse had two levels: its bottom was at the water's edge for boats, and its top was where I lived.

When I looked out the picture window overlooking Superior, I felt like I was on a ship. Ore boats and foreign vessels seemed to glide in front of me like so many toy boats, and I could hear the thump-thump of their engines passing. Some nights, northern lights danced over my "bridge."

On storm-filled nights, the spray was thrown high against my boat-house window, but some mornings, the big lake was so tranquil that the water seemed like a piece of glass. You could see down to the bottom.

On such a fine morning, when the lake was calm, and the sun shone above, I felt the most fabulous swimming hole in the world was right at my doorstep. An idea grew: I knew that this northernmost Great Lake was cold—bone-chilling frigid—but why shouldn't I try venturing into it with some protection?

I found a shop on the Duluth waterfront that handled SCUBA diving gear. I took the financial plunge. After unwrapping the yellow SCUBA suit in the boathouse, I examined it closely. The two-piece diving suit was constructed of rubber about the thickness of an old-fashioned inner tube. The top and bottom would cover me, from nose to toes.

The bottom included rubber feet, much like a baby's pajamas. The top of the diving suit had a hood. Hopefully, the top and the bottom could be rolled together in the suit's center into a watertight band. I would be snug and secure, encased in rubber.

I dressed thoughtfully. I began by sliding into my wool U.S. Army long johns and the wool sweater I had worn as an armored infantryman in Germany's "Black Forest" one winter during the Cold War. I pulled up Army wool socks that had kept me warm when I slept in the snow in my combat boots. I added a precaution for Superior: I pulled on another pair of socks.

The suit's bottom half slid on easily, including the rubber "booties," but I got into trouble as I tugged on the upper portion. The top pulled down over my head and shoulders without much resistance, but the rubbery mass would not unroll further.

Something was wrong. I could not roll it up or pull it further down. I was helpless, with my arms sticking up as if I were the victim of a holdup.

I shuffled up the embankment to the nearest house, waving my arms above my head. A teenage daughter saw me. "Mom... Mom!" she rushed off.

Moments later, Ms. Guido Gulder appeared at the door. She looked at her red-faced boathouse tenant encased in yellow rubber with his arms above his head, waving feebly.

"I'm having a minor problem," I tried to explain.

She turned away. I saw her shoulders shake as she seemed to hold a hand to her mouth. What was going on?

I bent over at the waist, extending my arms in front. "If you could just help get it off...."

I was sure I heard titters of laughter, but then I felt hands grab the suit. They tugged as I pulled backward.

Suddenly, the suit top was nearly off. It did not constrict me anymore. Or hold me up.

"Thanks," I said, picking myself off the ground.

As I tottered away with my yellow suit top partially off, I heard more laughter, not at all muffled by the kitchen door.

Days later, I worked up enough courage to again try my diving suit. Bright yellow all over, except for a red face and white hands, I picked my way down the rocky slope to the water's edge. Superior greeted the new frogman by throwing foam in his face. The lake was churning with quick-moving but small waves.

I paused. Should I press my luck?

Something made a noise behind me. I turned to glance up.

I had an audience. The family that had helped me a few days ago was lined up on the bank, waiting to see what their boathouse occupant was up to.

Attempting to look nonchalant, I eased my rubber-coated feet into the oncoming waves. I felt chill Superior pressing against my feet and then my legs.

Keep going! I urged myself. Almost floating, I walked into the surf until the waves were thigh-high. Then to my waist.

It was time. I sucked in a deep breath and, with a splash, tried to submerge. But my butt and legs floated up. And then the rest of me. The submerging part needed work.

Clambering back to shore, I heard a patter of applause. My audience was appreciative—and kind.

I had survived my first outing in my brand-new diving suit in Superior's chill waters. But I had a few kinks to work out.

When my workday ended, I'd hurry out of my editorial office in Duluth to my boathouse, climb into my diving suit and wade out into the lake. I found that I could float and splash around easily, but it was clear that I needed more equipment: a diving mask and a snorkel.

I did not know how to use them. I'd have to improvise sea trials.

I filled my bathtub, put on my mask and snorkel, and immersed my face in the water. It was an eerie feeling, having your head underwater and trying to breathe through a rubber tube.

With a gurgle, I heard the snorkel fill with water. I waited a moment— then blew hard. Water erupted from the snorkel onto my bathroom wall— the mask and snorkel worked fine.

I was ready.

On calm days, I would swim with my mask underwater and breathe through my snorkel to peer into Superior's depths as an occasional fish swam by. Below me, I saw dark, jagged rocks, and when I dove down to explore, I found pieces of wreckage and debris.

Sometimes, the lake was so clear that I felt like I was floating in air. Other times, the lake was leaden and dark. I could barely see my outstretched hand. Superior could be a portal to something dark and ominous.

With experience, I grew comfortable and secure in my diving suit but became aware of another problem. The air trapped in my wool army underwear and the rubber suit made me buoyant. It was challenging to get under the water—or stay below. I'd bob up.

I devised a plan: rear up in the water, do a jackknife dive, and plunge below headfirst to get underwater. Then swim hard to keep under the waves. Otherwise, I would float like a cork to the top of the water.

I had an excuse to visit the diving shop to buy more gear. I purchased a diver's belt of lead weights.

The first time out, I used all the weights on the weight belt. I sank and kept dropping until I started swimming hard to the surface. My weight belt needed fine-tuning.

Eventually, I learned to carry just enough weight to achieve neutral buoyancy, where I did not go up or down—just hung at whatever depth I wanted. It was like flying.

More equipment was needed: a pair of yellow flippers. Now I had power when I moved my legs in a scissors-like motion, up and down.

I added a diving knife that I attached to my right ankle. It had a heavy, long blade, serrated on one edge and sharp on the other. I had a tool to cut myself free if I got entangled in anything below. Besides, it looked sporty.

I was breaking the rules by going out alone, but as a practical matter, there was no one who wanted to go out with me from my lonely beach—especially on stormy days.

I compensated by taking along an old inner tube, which bobbed behind me in the water, tethered to my belt with a rope.

The tube was a drag. As I chugged in the water, it slowed me down and sapped my energy.

I began experimenting with smaller floatation. Two plastic milk gallon jugs would keep me up in my diving suit but were less bulk to drag around.

I graduated to smaller quart-size plastic bottles. A little floatation was all I needed to keep my head above water.

I finally arrived at the ultimate solution: No inner tubes, no sealed plastic bottles—only myself in my dry suit. It kept me up. Most importantly, I felt safe.

I grew bold. In stormy weather, I'd chug out from shore, lying in the water with my mask half submerged. I had the sensation of waves rushing toward me like walls of water. Seconds before they covered me, I took a deep breath through my snorkel—and let the waves slide over my head. Like a submarine, I was submerged. The world turned quiet. When the wave passed over me, I'd pop back up again and blow the water out through my snorkel. And enjoy a deep breath.

When I went out far enough, I found I could take a ride down the front of large waves if I timed them correctly. The wave would submerge me, pass over, and I would pop up, perched at their peak.

I began the scintillating ride down with a few flips of my flippers. I'd have to get a good breath of air in the trough before the next wave covered me again.

I'd begin the process all over again.

I did not have a surfboard. I surfed the waves on my belly—safely ensconced in my yellow suit.

I began venturing out alone on Superior after dark. In the night sky, the moon grew enormous over the waters. It painted the dark with a silver river. Stars twinkled in the skies, and sometimes above me, the northern lights began to writhe in their eerie dance.

Out here, the world had sounds and rhythms. And beauty. I grew to love this ancient, mysterious world. ❂

14

The Longboat Captain

A golden age on the big boats—and the
Edmund Fitzgerald

THE OLD CAPTAIN had taken me up on an invitation to visit my boat. I had spent several weeks in the Apostle Islands, hanging from the anchor and tying up at rustic docks, and now I was in the Duluth–Superior harbor at posh Barker's Island.

Captain Guido Gulder, even without his captain's hat, still looked every inch the Great Lakes big boat skipper he once was. A tall man in his seventies, he wore his age gracefully.

As he stepped aboard *Persistence,* I remembered how we met. He owned the North Shore boathouse I had been renting years ago—where I learned to skin dive. One evening he knocked on my screen door. His ore boat was in the Duluth loading docks; his car was in the garage, and Capt. Gulder needed to return quickly to his boat—would I give him a lift? I gathered it was an urgent matter.

Soon we were on board *James A. Farrell.* I had never been onboard an ore carrier, and I was amazed at its size and complexity.

The first mate came rushing up: "He's been drinking again,"

The captain shook his head sadly.

The fireman smelled of alcohol and weaved a little. The captain spoke gently, reminding the fireman that he had been warned about his drinking on duty. Company rules, the captain pointed out, strictly forbade alcohol consumption.

The fireman looked down. Yes, he had a bottle; yes, he was drinking. After a pause, the captain told the fireman he was released from service and had to get off the boat right now—company rules.

"I'm sorry," the captain said with regret. The fired fireman walked meekly away.

After forty-five years, the captain had retired from the longships. A surprise: I learned Captain Gulder and his family now lived in my old boathouse—the one I rented when I discovered my love of diving. He had moved out of his "big house" on top of the hill, taken the boathouse over, fixed it, and enlarged it.

I was pleased he had come down to the marina, but I had initially offered to meet him. I told him I'd sail over to the North Shore and anchor off the boathouse. I thought of drawing up the centerboard (with the board up, *Persistence* only drew six inches of water) and then wading to shore. *Huzza!* What a splendid idea. The long-lost writer returneth. The concept appealed to me to come "home" in this way.

"Don't do that."

"Why?"

"If a storm comes up, you'll lose your boat."

He added, "You know the area pretty well, don't you?" He reminded me of my hours underwater in my yellow diving suit.

Yes, I recalled. On the bottom, fronting the boathouse, lay rocks, big and small. I had two Danforth anchors on board, which work well in sand, gravel, bottom mud, and even, as I found out, taconite trailings—but not on large boulders. The flukes would not catch. I might go ashore and return to see my ship floating merrily out to the middle of Superior.

The sun was setting, burnishing everything golden in its long rays. The elderly captain took a seat across from me in the cockpit, and we began to talk. He spoke nostalgically of the old times on the lake, even though he worked twelve-hour days and earned an average of 27 ½ cents an hour.

When he began sailing the Great Lakes in 1930, ships were up to 600 feet long, carried about 11,000 to 12,000 tons, and had a draft of about 20 feet. But now, the longboats had increased to over a thousand feet in length and took on a whopping 63,000 tons. The ship's draft was 28 feet.

In the old days, the lakers, such as his *Farrell,* had proper quarters to carry passengers, always two and sometimes eight. Often the passengers were customers of the shipping company who received free passage.

"It was a privilege," he explained, "and it was a way to escape summertime heat." The voyages lasted seven days from Duluth to Conneaut, Ohio. Today, the longboats operate with fewer men, and their voyage duration is shorter: about five days.

The old ships never wore out. "A ship can keep going on," the captain said. "Those reciprocating engines run forever, so long as you reline their cylinder walls and take care of their bearings and shafts."

Captain Gulder became sad. "They were well built but slow."

"What happened to the old ships?"

"We must have sent one hundred of them to the scrapyard. And they ended up in foreign ports. I don't like it."

Was it hard to figure out what was happening in an old boat without today's electronic equipment? The thought crossed my mind that they might be so big that the crew would not know what was happening on their ship.

Captain Gulder shook his head. "It doesn't take long to know about a problem on a boat."

Including hitting a reef?

He knew what I was talking about. "In fair weather, if you were to touch bottom, you would know about it, and if damage occurred, the listing of the ship or the change in the draft would soon tell the men in charge," he said.

"Most times, when a ship touches the bottom, you can feel the rumble, little or big, depending on the damage, if any. However, under certain circumstances, such as during a storm, a captain might touch and not know about it," he said. "but the consequences would be known quickly."

Captain Guilder acknowledged that he had "rubbed on a few reefs" in his lengthy career.

He told me that when he was a mate in his younger days, his ship was running slowly in thick fog and strong current—and hit some boulders.

"What a ruckus that made," he said. "You *know* you hit bottom."

That brought to mind the *Edmund Fitzgerald.* One moment *Fitzgerald* had been in radio contact—the next, she was gone. It was as if the seas had suddenly swallowed up this 728-foot steel vessel.

I wondered aloud: Did the crew know they were sinking?

"Even if a longboat crew did not know the instant they hit, they would know if their boat was taking on water," he said.

So, yes, the crew knew.

Had *Fitzgerald* hit a reef? The waterfront talk had pinpointed what was referred to as Six Fathom Shoals near Caribou Island—the likely "touching" spot.

"It sticks out a long way, and others have hit it," Captain Gulder confirmed. "Most shippers feel the *Fitzgerald* touched. He was southerly." He meant that the big laker had strayed too far south in the storm, and in his track was the deadly reef.

Captain Gulder returned to his reminiscences. "At first, I was sorry to be off the lakes, but not now. When they had large fleets in the old days, there was lots of competition, but everyone had to cooperate. Now everything is different —cold and impersonal. You hardly have any human beings around compared to how it used to be."

And there was another matter: "Today, ships even have air conditioning." He seemed to sniff the air.

I managed a smile. That was one thing I did not have to worry about. My 20-foot sloop did not have air conditioning.

I heard rapid footsteps on the dock and looked up. Captain C. J. Porter, Master Mariner, Commander USCG (Retired), was a barrel-chested man with strong arms and a reddish face. He was cradling something in his arms.

"Nice little boat," he said. Somehow, he seemed to take charge.

He glanced at my compasses. I had a large bulkhead Gemini, a compass fitted atop my hatch cover, and even a compass over my berth—so I could glance up at night to see my boat's heading when I was at anchor.

"The weather is changeable up here," he warned. "And where you are going, iron masses will throw your compass off maybe ten degrees. If you haven't had your compasses swung, you could be off considerably."

"Now's as good a time as any," he added, stepping on board. "Especially if you're going up the North Shore."

No doubt about it: Captain Porter had taken charge. Captain Gulder smiled.

"How do we do this?"

"Head out. I'll tell you what direction I want you to go by your compass."

Under power, I headed *Persistence* into the harbor. There was a fine, fresh breeze blowing.

"Give me north by your compass," Captain Porter ordered. He was now hunched over his mysterious box, and I could see it held an expensive-looking gyrocompass. He was beginning to adjust my main Aqua Meter Gemini bulkhead compass.

"Sing out your heading," he said.

"North...north...north."

A moment later, the captain interrupted: "I need to feel confident."

I was not singing correctly. Or maybe just not loud enough.

"NORTH...NORTH...NORTH!"

That did it. I hunched forward to look over Captain Porter's shoulder as he worked on my compass in the tiny cockpit. It was more difficult than I had imagined for me to hold an exact, straight course.

"I don't feel confidence," he said. I had stopped repeating my headings.

"NORTH...NORTH...NORTH."

My eyes were glued to my bulkhead compass. *Persistence* bounded about, waves playfully slapping her bow just enough to make it difficult for me to hold course within a few compass degrees.

It took a lot of concentration. I concentrated.

Suddenly, I sat up straight, frantically looking around.

No one's watching the helm!

We were amid a busy harbor channel, with boats of all sizes speeding about. In the distance rumbled a massive ore carrier.

I had been concentrating on the compass—not watching for danger.

"Don't worry about a thing, boy," Captain Porter nodded to Captain Gulder.

I sat back. I realized my boat was being cared for by two grand old men who had spent their lives on Superior. I was not just in good company but in the best of company.

I got a new course. "West….west….west." I happily repeated.
It was a grand day for me and my boat in the Duluth–Superior Harbor.
I was now chock-full of confidence. ✻

15

Storm off the Shipwreck Coast

A sudden blow takes its best shot

THE FORECAST WAS FOR WINDS out of the southwest, steady 13 to 15 knots, with unlimited visibility. We'd be on a beam reach, a great point of sail for a 35-foot seagoing catamaran. The one to-two-feet waves would be no problem at all.

I opened my *Boat Log & Record,* as I was wont to do daily to fill out my sailing log. Each page had a bit of nautical poetry, doggerel, or salty wisdom to greet me. Today's message was: "Boats are safe in harbor, but that's not what boats are for."

Odd, but that sounded more ominous than was called for on a bright, sunshiny day with a clear forecast.

I shrugged my shoulders: this was Superior.

I took over the helm as skipper Joe and his son, Bruce, hoisted the canvas. I could feel the sails catch the wind and billow with power; the big cat surged forward. This was what I had been waiting for: a high-speed run.

It was a steady, upright ride, as if we were on rails. If I had been sailing my 20-foot boat, we'd have a lively ride as *Persistence's* shoulder dug in and went to work—the tippy, bouncy way a monohull was designed to be sailed. It was a symphony of movement between wind, water, and waves. But the wide-beamed cat stayed upright and responded to wind gusts by moving faster ahead.

I watched, fascinated as the knot meter piled up ever higher numbers. I saw 7…8…8.2 knots.

I was alone at the helm, watching the compass and adjusting course as the growing gusts hit the sails. Checking the digital knotmeter and then the GPS, I saw that our speed didn't fall below 6½ knots but quickly could run up to about 8 knots in a gust.

We were doing well for a heavy cruising cat.

To starboard lay the beautiful Pictured Rocks, an area where Ojibwa tradition held that gods lived. It was not difficult to understand why looking at the spectacular cliffs and getting the awesome feeling of nature.

The Pictured Rocks area was spun into poetry by Henry Wadsworth Longfellow in his *Song of Hiawatha.* It was here that Hiawatha:

> *Heard the whispering of the pine-trees,*
> *Heard the lapping of the waters,*
> *Sounds of music, worlds of wonder.*

I remember as a schoolboy thrilling to the lines:

> *By the shores of Gitche Gumee,*
> *By the shining Big-Sea-Water,*
> *Stood the wigwam of Nokomis…*
> *Dark behind it rose the forest,*
> *Rose the black and gloomy pine-trees,*
> *Rose the firs with cones upon them.*
> *Bright before it beat the water,*
> *Beat the clear and sunny water,*
> *Beat the shining Big-Sea-Water.*

As we sailed the Big-Sea-Water, I kept checking the knotmeter and saw our speed edging upwards. The cat was tearing across the wave trains.

It was getting windy out here, and I glanced toward the open waters. The waves were capped with white.

Whitecaps! We were getting more than the steady, mild forecast winds—a squall seemed to be coming our way.

The cat only settled down when the gusts hit and sizzled faster across the waves.

Time after time, I'd play the gusts. The steering had a light touch to it now, and I had to concentrate not to oversteer.

I heard a roaring in my ears. A gust of wind hit, and the cat took off. We skittered across the wave trains, the two hulls straddling them.

Then came a trough between the speeding waves. The two hulls could not straddle them, and we dipped, first one hull, then the other. The hulls dug in the waves hard and noisily.

Bam! There was a jolt that ran through the boat. Spray flew back, splashing me. The hulls were pitching hard.

"Some squall," Joe drawled.

"I'd say we have gusts to 50 knots," Thom, the ex-navy man, observed. "Look at the waves."

Sure enough, the waves had grown larger, with troughs that let one hull dip down while the other went skyward a few feet.

We were getting slammed about in a gut-jarring ride, but the boat seemed to be handling rough conditions with confidence-enhancing aplomb. In fact, the faster we went, the better the cat rode, leveling off lesser waves as she plunged ahead.

We vibrated, with stresses building on the two hulls and the bridge deck as they encountered the harsh seas.

I glanced up at the mainsail. It had a weird shape, like it was being bent outward and twisted at an odd, not happy, angle. It had developed a distinct bulge, like a giant balloon.

The boat stayed upright on two hulls. Since the hulls did not lean, the sail took the wind's force.

"Time to reef," Joe said.

Thom took over the wheel as I went forward with Joe.

We needed to get some sail down, and the cat was designed with a system that would let us reef the mainsail from inside the cockpit. I could identify the colored line that led from the boom, through turning blocks, to the line clutch atop the cabin's aft bulkhead.

One pull—a device like a big roller shade would revolve—and down would drop the main, battens and all, to be stored inside the boom. You could reef as much sail as you wanted. It just would wind around the in-boom furling device.

"Let this out slowly," Joe told me. I grabbed the halyard that would keep tension on the main. Joe uncleated the reefing line and gave it a hearty tug.

Nothing happened.

"Give me some slack." He put his 200-plus heft into the reefing line.

Nothing budged. The sail was stuck.

We lurched atop another tumbling wave, one hull digging in. The hull groaned.

"Take hold of the furling line." He moved to the cabin top, where he clung to the mast.

"Pull!"

But the sail would not come down. Joe attempted manually to force the sail into the awaiting furler.

The sail was equipped with full-length battens—fiberglass strips that ran horizontal to the boom. The wind's substantial force had bent them to one side; their curves would not fit into the narrow slot.

"Give me some slack," Joe yelled. I let out the rope clutch, presumably allowing the sail to fall. It did not.

Surprise, surprise. One more thing was going wrong at the worst possible time.

Exasperated, Joe reached high to grab a handful of sail. Then another. He wrestled the mainsail down by hand and folded it atop the boom. He wrapped a line around both.

It didn't look elegant, but it worked. The flapping sail was now off the mast and secured to the boom.

Jumping back into the cockpit, Joe grabbed the furling line to the jib, flying on a jib furler. "It's a Harken. You know this will work."

With a smooth, steady pull, the jib rolled up. The boat settled down and moved under diesel power.

Joe and Thom consulted the charts. Though the shoreline looked fierce—this was the Shipwreck Coast—there were few shoals offshore. The underwater contours showed deepening waters without obstructions.

The cat drew only a few feet. We would do as the voyageurs in birch-bark canoes did in a storm: head for the windward shore.

We crept closer. The whitecaps diminished, and the waves thinned down. The high cliffs took the brunt of the wind's blast.

We closely watched our depth sounder, keeping our boat in about 25 to 30 feet of water. That allowed plenty of water beneath our hulls. We motored along at six and a half knots—not what we were doing under sail in the gusts. But we were playing it a lot safer.

Boating was a pleasure again. We zipped in close to the shores of the Grand Sable Sand Dunes.

Odd, I thought as I glanced toward the land. We were cruising on the edge of the north woods primeval, with some of the oldest rocks in the world, on the biggest lake in the world. Now it appeared as if we were sailing in the Sahara Desert.

Massive dunes towered along the shore. One bluff rose 300 feet, with 35 degrees of incline. I could see the wind gusts make sandy swirls on the dune-colored bank.

"It's smoking up there," Joe observed.

It was an impressive beach scene, but with no beachgoers. No one was there to risk the wind or dip their toes into the lake's chill waters. I did not blame them.

With the lift from the storm's high winds, we were ahead of our estimated arrival time at the small-craft harbor of Grand Marais, Michigan. But as we entered the breakwaters, I saw that places to tie a boat along a pier or bulkhead were already taken by earlier arrivals, mostly powerboats.

We circled the public dock. No luck at all. The boats were jammed in, bow to stern.

Heading out again, we began to maneuver around the harbor, searching. We wove around several sailboats, then headed for the western shore. We'd anchor out.

From our charts, we knew that the bottom was sand—good holding for our anchors. We cruised back and forth 200 yards from the windward shore, using our depth sounder to determine the amount of water we had under our twin hulls.

I went forward with Joe and dropped both a large Danforth and a CQR plow-type anchor in a "v" pattern. Thom backed the cat to test that the anchors were holding and that we had plenty of scope should a heavy blast come through.

Our concern was not that the anchors wouldn't do the job—they were oversized and could hold a much larger boat—but that if the wind shifted, as Lake Superior winds are apt to do, we'd still have enough water under our hulls if our position changed.

An 11,000-pound catamaran would be tough to kedge off a beach.

The wind swirled eddies in the harbor, making our cat dance from side to side. For a few moments, I thought that the anchors were dragging. Yet, I realized there was no way that the CQR and the Danforth would do anything but burrow deeper into the sand bottom, holding us securely.

Behind us, riding easily at anchor, I saw an older-looking sloop with a white-bearded skipper. We were about 100 feet apart, and both boats swung to and fro in the gusts.

"Are we coming too close?"

"It's your boat." The skipper smiled amiably, shrugged his shoulders, and went below.

I studied the motion of the two boats, and it appeared at least we were not getting any nearer. The depth sounder confirmed that we held steady at about 12 feet. Had we slipped nearer the anchored boat, that number would have gone up.

Joe turned on the anchor lights. We were set for the night, anchored and secure. Going below, we assembled in the cat's lounge with wrap-around portlights. We enjoyed the lowering light in the west and the darkening shore. It was a glorious sunset.

Darkness came, and the cat tugged at her anchors, swaying back and forth with the wind gusts. From my bunk in the main salon, I felt every motion. It was not unpleasant, like being in a hammock in a tree, pleasantly rocked back and forth.

I fell asleep. Hours later, I awakened, listening. Something was different.

There was no low moan from the mast and rigging. The boat was not cocking back and forth.

I jumped out of my sleeping bag, threw open the hatch, and stepped on deck.

The northern air was fresh and chill. The moon had risen and had become a giant white orb. Off to the north, I could see the northern lights winking against the dark sky.

I turned my head, trying to feel the wind's direction on my face and ears: it still blew out of the east, but it had moderated a lot.

I padded forward in my bare feet to the bow, then reached down to tug at the anchor lines. They seemed firm enough, under constant tension. That meant the anchors were holding.

All was well. I ambled back to my bunk and pulled up my sleeping bag. Tomorrow would be another day on mighty Superior. ❄

16

The Shipwreck Museum

Treasures interpret Superior's heroic past

IT WAS BLOWING 30 KNOTS as we entered the breakwaters at the harbor of refuge about a mile southwest of Whitefish Point. We were getting off the notorious Shipwreck Coast—sometimes called "the graveyard of the Great Lakes."

I had an old chart showing where each wreck occurred and where it lay underwater. This lake section was the worst for shipping casualties—more than 200, many of which are still lost in the depths. The "graveyard" extended to Munising—an 80-mile stretch of inhospitable shores in our wake. I was glad to be heading for port.

The Whitefish Point Harbor of Refuge had only nine slips used by local boaters and commercial fishermen. We were in luck: one slip was open. But the slip was only about 17 feet wide. Our cat was 15 feet wide.

One foot clearance on either side—in gusty crosswinds.

Thom Burns, an ex-Navy man, took the helm and began maneuvering the craft forward. I noticed that water exited under the hull in unusual streams. He was using the cat's engines in a maneuver with counter-rotating screws. One screw was forward, the other in reverse. Thom set up a combination that would give him control of the boat sideways and point in various directions to overcome the crosswinds.

The diesels thrummed, the hull inched ahead, and finally, we were in the slip with about a foot to spare on either side.

"I knew you could do it," the skipper said. Thom looked relieved.

I helped cross-tie the cat between the outer wall and several pilings. Our boat was secure for the night.

As afternoon shadows lengthened, I hiked out of the marina and onto a gravel road to the Point. The day was pleasant on this peninsula, sticking deep into Superior. The air was fresh. Birds sang in the deep woods that overshadowed our path. The occasional car whizzed past.

Ahead jutted the unmistakable shape of the 1861 Whitefish Point Lighthouse (a national historic site), which has been in operation since the U.S. Civil war when Abraham Lincoln was the president of the United States. Around it clustered several other buildings, all in white, tucked behind the dunes. Standing upright from the sands was an ancient wooden rudder that must have been 25 feet high.

A sign proclaimed this was the Great Lakes Shipwreck Museum.

As I entered, three SCUBA divers hovered over the bones of a wreck as they hung from the ceiling. I moved closer, fascinated by the realistic wreck display.

Suddenly, I realized that this was no stage prop but the actual timbers from the sunken *Independence,* the first steamship on Lake Superior. She blew up in a boiler explosion in 1816. These were *Independence's* actual frames, ribs, and planks—the museum had rescued them from their 150-year underwater slumber.

Here was one of the best displays of preserved underwater artifacts and history I had seen—and I appreciated the respectful use of the wreck fragments that once lay unseen on Superior's dark bottom.

What a price the early mariners paid to ply the waters of this lake. Some were lost in devastating gales; some met their end in fog-shrouded collisions. They had fought wild and mountainous seas and billowing black water. Ice. Sub-zero cold.

Some are still out there, beneath the waves.

Thomas Farnquist started SCUBA diving in 1972 and became obsessed with the sport. He was a science instructor, teaching school during

L.) The actual bell of the sunken *Edmund Fitzgerald* was recovered, restored and now stands proudly in the main hall of the Shipwreck Museum. C.) From the depths, an ancient windship anchor. R.) A display counter shows retrieved underwater objects in front of a wall with ship's wheels from *Superior City* and *John B. Cowle,* which sank by collision around Whitefish Point.

Photos/ The Great Lakes Shipwreck Museum.

the winter but spending summers following his passion: searching for and diving on underwater wrecks along the Shipwreck Coast. He and his diving partners located 25 "virgin"—previously unlocated and untouched— sunken wrecks.

In 1978, he founded the Great Lakes Shipwreck Historical Society and began the Shipwreck Memorial Museum beside the historic lighthouse. Visitors drove a lonely road along the peninsula to reach the sandy tip jutting into Superior. The museum is located 11 miles north of Paradise, the nearest community, and is 33 miles from Highway 28.

Farnquist's dream grew. In 1983, the society signed a long-term lease and began rebuilding and restoring former U.S. Lighthouse Service and Coast Guard buildings. Later, it added the automated 1860s-era lighthouse.

"We saw artifacts disappearing—and we wanted to keep them at Whitefish Point or at least in Michigan," he told me.

He explained that some SCUBA divers pillaged wrecks in earlier decades to bring back souvenirs of their dives. However, in 1980, state law prohibited amateur divers from taking anything from the ships they found on the bottom. Now only museums can remove selected items—only after obtaining a permit. They must also develop a salvage plan, a conservation plan, and a public exhibition schedule.

"The vast majority of people will never visit shipwrecks," Farnquist

The museum's *David Boyd* heads out on a search mission. The twin-diesel boat is equipped with the latest in underwater research technology.

Photo/ The Great Lakes Shipwreck Museum.

told me, explaining his vision of the museum. "Some artifacts representing shipboard life or identifiable from a vessel should be recovered if there is a good conservation plan and a plan for proper exhibition and care. We would not want to recover everything from a wreck, only a few select artifacts that represent the human history and the uniqueness of the vessel. This wouldn't take away the vessel's integrity as a dive site for other divers."

As a SCUBA diver, I wondered how he found the wrecks. He told me he began by researching early newspaper accounts and then "putting an x on the chart" where he calculated the wrecks might be located. After that, he systematically searched the bottom aboard his dive boat, primarily using side-scan sonar.

So that Farnquist and his divers could get to and from a potential wreck site, the Society revamped a 40-foot Coast Guard picket boat, powered by two 671 diesel engines, with a top speed of about 20 mph.

"When we acquired the boat from the Coast Guard, it was bare-bones, and the engines were tired," he said. The Society had them rebuilt and upgraded to add 50 more horsepower. They repainted the steel hull and added electronics, including through-hull sonar scanners, so Farnquist and his divers could quickly search an area.

Over the years, the ex-Coast Guard vessel proved to be a good sea boat. "We've outrun several storms," Farnquist said, "but we had to run for our lives at times. One year we had unusual storms in July out of the northwest. Around here, the storm we dread is the northwester since that sweeps over the lake's entire length, building up waves on this end.

"We had waves that were 10-to-15 feet high. We tried to run, but the following sea came too quickly, running over our fantail. We couldn't make it back to the protection of Whitefish Point, so the only thing to do was to take the waves on the quarter and run for Little Lake Harbor, about 12 miles west of Whitefish Point. We made it OK, though, with difficulty.

"If you are on this lake long enough there will come a time when you'll have trouble getting off it and into a safe harbor."

How did this section of Lake Superior get to be "The Graveyard of the Great Lakes?" Farnquist told me that of the 550 shipwrecks on Lake Superior, the Shipwreck Coast accounts for 150 to 200, "depending on what you measure."

Most shipwrecks occurred around the turn of the century and involved accidents in which some boats were recovered. Other shipwrecks were total losses, with calamitous loss of life, and the ships were still on the bottom. Some vessels disappeared into the lake and were never located, though evidence of their passing, such as bits and pieces of the boats, eventually washed up onshore.

The *Myron* was one of the Shipwreck Coast's worst accidents.

It had been a bitter November 1919 when the 186-foot-long lumber hooker *Myron* was caught in the shipmasters' nightmare, a black north-wester. November is the most dangerous time for vessels on Superior's open waters; during these last runs before shipping ends, the lake can lash out with quick-rising gales.

With decks piled high with rough lumber, the 676-ton wooden hooker had departed Munising, Michigan, bound for Buffalo. When the northwester hit, hard waves mauled Myron and began to spring her planks and make her leak.

The battered Myron lost power about a mile northwest of Whitefish Point. Water crept up Myron's bilges, extinguishing her boiler's fires. Her steam-driven engine halted, and Myron wallowed in the battering waves.

Capt. Walter F. Neal ordered the 16-man crew to launch her two lifeboats. Four minutes later, Myron sank. As dark waters closed over her, the piles of rough lumber on her decks wrenched free. The wave-tossed log-jam slammed into the two lifeboats, threatening to sink them.

The steel ore carriers, *Adriatic* and *H.P. McIntosh,* saw *Myron's* plight and drove toward the wreckage. The *Adriatic* stood off, but the *McIntosh* edged close enough to throw lines to the ice-coated survivors in the lifeboats. But the men in the numbing water could not catch and hold the icy lines. *McIntosh* withdrew in danger from being stove in by the pounding timbers in the waves. *Myron's* crew could only watch in despair as the rescue ship pulled away, unable to help them.

In the meantime, a lifeboat crew from the life-saving station at Vermillion Point pursued the *Myron* on the heavy seas. After several heavy thumps, the Life Savers gave up the chase. They decided that their small wooden lifeboat could not survive the battering of the wave-tossed lumber.

After ordering his crew to get off the sinking ship and into lifeboats, Capt. Neal climbed to *Myron's* pilothouse, slammed the door behind him, and dogged it shut. He had decided to go down with his ship.

As he stood behind the wheel, the waters rose in front of him. He felt the frigid chill waters on his feet, then his chest, and he waited for his fate as the glass windows shattered from the pressure of the water.

Suddenly, he splashed atop the waves.

The pilothouse roof had burst off—and Captain Neal pulled himself atop the floating debris.

From his wave-washed roof-raft, he saw his crew members pounded by the churning lumber jam and become entombed in ice. All he could do was watch. For 20 hours, he was blown about. Then fate took a hand.

A steamer crisscrossed the icy waters in Whitefish Bay, searching for bodies. The steamer's captain hoisted his binoculars and saw something lying atop a piece of low-lying wreckage. It was the half-frozen Captain Neal.

They pulled him on board, suffering from exposure and hypothermia. He was safe, but the lifeboats his crew had set off in were nowhere to be found.

Eventually, *Myron's* sixteen crewmembers, clad in their ice-coated life jackets, were recovered from the beach. They were all frozen—and dead.

The worst collision in Lake Superior's history happened four miles from Whitefish Point a year later. At twilight, August 20, 1920, *Superior City*, filled with iron ore out of Two Harbors, Minnesota, neared the track of the fast steamer, the upbound *Willis L. King*. Lookouts on both vessels reported their sightings to their skippers; the boats exchanged signals. One sounded a port passing; the other starboard.

Capt. Edward Sawyer realized that the vessels were on a collision course. He swung his boat away and sounded the alarm.

But it was too late: *Willis L. King* rammed *Superior City*, punching a hole in her port side. The crew raced to the stern section where the lifeboats were kept. But *Superior's* icy waters got there first, slamming into the stricken vessels' red-hot boilers. *Superior City* exploded—tearing away the stern section and hurtling the crew into the air.

Within two minutes, *Superior City* sank beneath the waves, with the loss of 29 lives. Only four crew members were saved.

On November 24, 1918, three steel minesweepers, built at Fort William, Ontario, Canada, sailed out of Thunder Bay on the northern shores of Lake Superior. They were under the command of French Naval Lieutenant De Vaisseux Leclerc, who took the lead on board *Sebastopol*.

All three French Navy vessels had Lake Superior pilots on board. Their orders were to sail across Superior, make passage through the Great Lakes, and cross the North Atlantic to France.

The new 143-foot minesweepers were designed and built for heavy weather sailing on the world's oceans. Each vessel displaced 630 tons, had a beam of 22½ feet, drew 13½ feet, and had four watertight compartments. Their top speed was around 12 knots; each minesweeper was armed with two heavy four-inch guns, one forward and one aft.

But 24 hours out of Thunder Bay, the minesweepers encountered a Superior gale. A blizzard blinded them, then separated them. *Sebastapol* headed around Keweenaw Point for protection. The seas were so heavy that several of *Sebastapol's* welds broke and she was taking on water. The pumps ran continuously.

Lieutenant Leclerc and *Sebastapol* limped into the Soo locks on November 26 and waited for the rest of the fleet. They were in for an extended stay.

The other two minesweepers had disappeared.

An extensive search of Canadian and U.S. shores found no trace of the missing vessels or 76-man crews and Canadian pilots. It was as if the steel ships had fallen into a hole in Superior. Later stories speculated that the missing minesweepers had entered a northern version of the Bermuda Triangle, into which, legend has it, ships sail and never return.

Today some historians surmise that heavy seas brought down the minesweepers near the Keweenaw Peninsula. Farnquist thinks the vessels might lie anywhere between the Keweenaw and Whitefish.

Farnquist researched the vessels' voyage the same way he did other wrecks and listened to tales of fishermen and others who worked on the lake. He noted that an unpainted lifeboat drifted ashore along the Shipwreck Coast. It might have been off one of the French vessels.

Another clue came when a fisherman told about a human skeleton found on Michipicoten Island, northwest of Whitefish Point. It wore a tattered French naval officer's uniform.

The ill-fated French vessels may lie somewhere on the bottom, between the rugged shipwreck coast and the island to the north.

"Imagine finding the minesweepers complete with their cannon down in the depths," Farnquist said.

Another mystery of Superior is the disappearance of the "Flying Dutchman of Superior," the 245-foot steamer *Bannockburn.* The 1,620-ton steel steamer was built in Great Britain in 1893 and sailed the Atlantic. On November 20, 1902, she was on a late run out of Port Arthur, Ontario, with her hull filled with 85,000 bushels of Canadian wheat.

A mid-Lake Superior storm caught her. Two Canadian ships reported sighting *Bannockburn* northeast of the Keweenaw Point, heading eastward; that was the last anyone saw her. Her 20-man crew disappeared with her.

Farnquist notes that wreckage, including a life jacket bearing the ship's name, washed up on the shores near Grand Marais. *Bannockburn* may lie somewhere off the Shipwreck Coast.

Whitefish Point came to be known as "Shipwreck Point" because it is the entrance to the Shipwreck Coast. Farnquist explained that Whitefish marks the turning point for all ships, either entering or leaving Whitefish Bay—where shipping lanes come dangerously close. There were a lot of collisions in fog, storms, and even smoke from forest fires.

"There was nowhere to hide in the storms," he points out, "except at Whitefish Point or Grand Marais, difficult to get into. Remember, too, that there are 350 miles of open lake, and the prevailing winds are out of the northwest, especially in November, when so many ships run into trouble."

I walked past the historic lighthouse—the light that failed one tragic night—and over the dunes to the water's edge.

A chill wind greeted me. From here, I could see far out into Superior. I tried to make out the approximate position where *Edmund Fitzgerald* sank on November 10, 1975, only 17 miles out. She was that close to safety.

Her captain and crew tried to find this shore through the storm-lashed lake. I knew they had been looking desperately for this tip of land and the lighthouse, probably right where I stood.

They never made it. *Fitzgerald* still lies under 500 feet of water with her captain and crew. Their bodies have never been recovered. ✸

17

The Snowshoe Priest

"Paddle on—straight on. We must get through."

"It was a sight to arouse pity to see poor Frenchmen in a Canoe, amid rain and snow, borne hither and thither by whirlwinds in these great Lakes, which often show waves as high as those of the Sea. The men frequently found their hands and feet frozen upon their return, while occasionally, they were overtaken by so thick a fall of powdery snow, driven against them by a violent wind, that the one steering the Canoe could not see his companion in the bow. How then gain the port? Verily as often as they reached the land, their doing so seemed a little miracle."—Jesuit writer

TULLAMORE DEW'S twin diesels hummed happily at 2,800 rpm to give us a cruising speed of 6.8 knots. Today, we were on our way under technicolor scenery up the Keweenaw waterway's historic and beautiful water road.

We'd sail across historic Portage Lake, exit the waterway into the Keweenaw Bay and enter the open waters of Lake Superior. Then we'd sail past the Huron Islands along the rugged Michigan coast and, if all went well, end up in Marquette by late afternoon.

We were on the old route Native Americans and voyageurs used during the fur-trading era. We'd also be following the track of Lake Superior's famous "black robes," the French Missionaries Father Rene Menard and Father Frederic Baraga.

As a crew member of a modern catamaran, I enjoyed the comforts of the 35-foot boat. But the early voyageurs traveled by birchbark canoe, which Henry W. Longfellow rhapsodized as floating upon the water "like a yellow autumn leaf, like a yellow water lily."

"Extremely poetical," sniffed German writer Johann Georg Kohl in 1855, who also paddled through these waters. To him, a birchbark canoe was a "wretched fragile 'water lily,' made of thin birchbark, without the slightest comfort, no bench or support, nor even a bundle of hay or straw."

I leaned back in the cockpit's plush cushions, enjoying the scenery passing by. I could almost picture Kohl paddling grumpily in these waters, with an Ojibway lexicon in his backpack, collected by a black-robed priest known as the Snowshoe Priest.

The day was warm, almost tropical. The scenery glided by until about 11 a.m. when we entered Keweenaw Bay and Superior's open waters. I looked forward to getting under sail; the wind was forecast to come from the south to the southwest, which would mean fine sailing for the cat.

My thoughts turned back to Kohl, who reacted differently when his birch-bark canoe party entered the bay, worrying whether they would find a "vent de terre" or a "vent du large." Kohl wrote:

"We desired the former, for as these small voitures (canoes) always glide along near the shore, like timid ducks, the wind blowing offshore (vent de terre) is preferable for them. As it has to cross the steep shore cliffs and the forest, it strikes the lake some distance off, and leaves along the coast a perfectly smooth patch of water, over which the canoe glides rapidly. On the other hand, the "vent du large" sends up high waves, produces a violent surf, and renders a canoe voyage often impossible."

We didn't find either, for the wind perversely switched to the east—nearly on our cat's nose. The skipper made his decision: up sails, anyway.

We hoisted the big mainsail, then rolled out the genoa. With a pop, it caught the wind, and we cranked the big foresail down hard and set it taut with the winch.

We were motor sailing; the diesels idled along while the sails gave us a slight boost. We had created our own "vent," making an easy crossing of Keweenaw Bay, heading around Point Abbeye, a small point of land to the southeast.

The entry to the waterway from the east was where explorers Pierre Esprit Radisson and Medard Chouart, Sieur des Grosevilliers, paddled their birch-bark canoes in 1659. They had come from Sault St. Marie and were heading deeper into the wilderness of the Keweenaw Peninsula and then on to the Minnesota North Shore, where a river still bears the name of Grosevilliers. Today it is anglicized almost beyond reason as "Gooseberry River."

Radisson's account of his adventures became a best-selling book in its day, and Europeans must have been agog at this glimpse of the new world. Superior's shores were "most delightful and wounderous," with part of its south shore rocks like "a great Portall, by reason of the beating of the waves. The lower part of that opening is as bigg as a tower."

Elated with all he saw, he wrote: "We weare Cesars being nobody to contradict us."

But the Frenchman was not the first European to paddle through this remote area. Years before, Etienne Brule was sent to explore the new country. From the Hurons, he heard of a "sea of which they have not seen the end, nor heard that anyone has."

In 1623, Brule and his canoe party were believed to have crossed Superior and reached the Minnesota north shore. The Frenchman reported visiting a place on Superior where the Native Americans were mining copper and brought back an ingot of copper from a region "eighty or one hundred leagues from the Huron Country." (A league is about three miles.) Brule estimated the length of the great lake was "four hundred leagues."

Brule never returned to live in New France. As the story goes, his Lake Superior experience so changed Brule that he turned his back on European society and went to live with the Hurons, where he was killed in a knife fight over a woman. They ate his heart— a great honor.

The earliest "black robe" to come into this area, Father Rene Menard, also braved the Superior wilderness. Aging and in ill health, the French missionary had begun his journey in 1660 from New France in Canada (near Montreal) in a fleet of about 60 canoes paddled by Ottawas. His task was to gain converts among the Hurons who lived along the shores of Lake Superior.

Paddling up the St. Lawrence River, they followed the traditional canoe route that led past Montreal. They switched to the Ottawa River, then paddled and portaged rivers and streams to Georgian Bay. From there, they found Lake Superior.

The canoe party forced the elderly priest to both paddle and carry packs, Father Menard slipped at one of the many portages, injuring his foot and arm. He went barefoot for the rest of the trip because his foot had become infected and swollen.

Following the south shore of Superior, the canoe band hugged the land so they could pull their canoes off in case of sudden storms. When a falling tree destroyed the old priest's canoe, the rest of the party paddled away, leaving the old priest and his party stranded without food.

Father Menard and his group survived by making stews from bones and dried blood they found around an old campsite. Finally, another band of voyageurs paddled by and gave them a ride.

They voyaged past the Huron Mountains and into Keweenaw Bay, arriving on Saint Theresa's Day, October 15, 1660. Father Menard named the area after the saint, L'Anse de Sainte Therese, later shortened to L'Anse, meaning "cove."

He had spent 48 days on his journey, but the weary and injured priest was not yet at rest. The Ottawas ordered him away from their camp. He had to spend the winter in a hut he made of fir branches.

Father Menard managed to baptize 50 inhabitants, but nine months later, he decided to follow an ancient Indian trail to another village. His Huron guides deserted him on the way, and the elderly priest was never heard from again.

We headed further into Keweenaw Bay. Traverse Island lay to the north of us and further to the east, the Huron Islands that Father Menard canoed past. One of these islands may have given rise to the legend of Lake Superior's "disappearing islands." Author Kohl wrote:

"There lay a tall, bluish island, with which the mirage played in an infinity of ways during our voyage. At times, the island rose in the air to a spectral height, then sank again and faded away, while at another moment, we saw these islands hovering over one another in the air. That the watchful Indians not only observe this optical delusion but also form a correct idea of its cause, is provided by the name they give to the mirage. They call it *ombanitewin,* a word meaning…"something that swells and rises in the air."

I was reminded of the phenomenon when I stood on Minnesota's North Shore and looked over Superior's open waters. The distance faded into a light blue haze—nothing out there but water.

Surprise! Overnight, something had materialized boldly in the distance. I was gazing at Isle Royale, the largest island on Lake Superior, about 45 miles in length and 20 miles from Minnesota's shore. One day it was not there; the next, it was.

But it was not only the optical tricks of Superior that caused problems for the early explorers. I had to smile as I recalled that to the north and west of us supposedly lay Isle Phelipeaux. Decades of explorers had searched for this elusive island, which appeared first on a map drawn by a Parisian mapmaker. Isle Phelipeaux was situated off the Keweenaw Peninsula to the north, not far from Isle Royale. The mysterious island would have been hard to miss—on the map, Isle Phelipeaux was drawn nearly as large as Isle Royale.

Years later, it was learned that the French mapmaker had courted the favor of a patron named Phelipeaux. Lake Superior was so far from civilization, and such a wilderness, that if he were to draw in an extra island to honor his patron, who was to know? The bogus map confused searchers for years until it was discovered that this island was but a figment of a conniving mapmaker's imagination.

On top of red rock bluffs one mile west of L'Anse, Michigan, in a beautifully wooded area, rose a massive statue of a priest, his face turned to look down over the body of water we were cruising.

The golden 35-foot-tall figure gleamed brightly in the sunlight, supported on curved wooden beams resting on a base of concrete teepees, each about 10-feet-tall. The face is meditative, as if in prayer. The statue holds a cross in one massive hand and snowshoes in the other.

The Shrine of the Snowshoe Priest of Lake Superior is erected to honor Father Frederic Baraga's historic missionary work.

I had first heard of the Snowshoe Priest when I sailed to Madeline Island, where he had worked among the Ojibway of Superior and established the first permanent Catholic mission. Born in Austria of nobility, he had heard the church's call and was ordained after receiving his law degree at the University of Vienna. Fascinated by Native Americans, he had requested an assignment on Lake Superior, where he wrote what became best-selling books in Europe about Superior and Native American culture. He spent about 30 years on Superior traveling about the lake by snowshoe, dog team, and birchbark canoe.

He traveled widely—and fearlessly.

When Father Baraga was on Madeline Island, he received word that his immediate presence was needed at a mission on the northern side of the lake along the Minnesota North Shore.

Dressed as usual in his black robe with a gold cross on his chest, breviary in his hand, and a three-corner hat on his head, Father Baraga hurried to the hut of voyageur Louis Goudin. He probably also carried one or two raw potatoes in his cloak—his usual lunch.

It was 1846, and there were no roads along the shoreline or in the Sawtooth Mountains. An overland journey would take over a month. But the distance would be only 40 miles straight across the lake—if they made it.

The voyageur grew concerned. The weather did not look promising. The usual voyaging procedure was to stay close to the coast, travel to the head of the lake (later known as Duluth), and then paddle up the North Shore. If the weather got bad, the paddlers got off. They would pull their boats ashore, turn them over and live under them until the weather cleared.

But no one had attempted a crossing straight from the Apostles to the North Shore—all open water.

Father Baraga prevailed. The voyageur's boat was an 18-foot birch bark canoe. The good father sat in the middle, probably bailing water since the "bundle of twigs" were notorious leakers. The voyageur sat in the aft section, paddling.

From Madeline Island, they paddled to the outermost island in the Apostles. From Sand Island, they could look out on the big waters toward the North Shore. Kohl's book records a voyageur retelling the story of their voyage:

"It grew stormy, and the water rose in high waves. My cousin remarked that he had prophesied this, but his pious, earnest passenger read on in his breviary quietly and only now and then addressed a kind word of encouragement to my cousin. They toiled all night through the storm and waves, and, as the wind was fortunately with them, they moved along very rapidly, although their little bark danced like a feather on the waters.

In the morning, they could see land. But it was not a welcoming shore—full of rocks and reefs, topped with heavy surf. "It was the surf of the terribly excited waves. There was no opening in them, no heaven, no salvation."

"We are lost, your reverence," my cousin said, "it is impossible for me to keep the canoe balanced in these double and triple breakers."

"Paddle on—straight on. We must get through, and a way will offer itself."

The voyageur said his prayers and paddled on. Ahead, he heard the surf booming, and soon, they could not hear each other because of the noise. As they neared the dark shore, the waves grew worse.

Suddenly, "a dark spot opened in the white edge of the surf, which soon widened. At the same time, the violent heaving of the canoe relaxed; it glided on more tranquilly and entered in perfect safety the broad mouth of a stream, which they had not seen in the distance, owing to the rocks that concealed it."

The priest said, "Did I not say that I was called across, that I must go, and that thou wouldst be saved with me?"

They drew their canoe ashore, knelt on the rocks, and kissed the ground. The priest and the voyageur went into the forest, cut down several trees, and erected a cross where they landed to remember what had happened. After giving thanks and proclaiming their crossing a miracle, the two men walked northward along an old Indian trail to Grand Portage, where Father Baraga ministered to his Ojibway community.

The area became known as the Cross of Baraga's Traverse. Now it is simply "Baraga's Cross."

I first saw Father Baraga's Cross as I sailed along the North Shore, heading northward from Duluth to Canada. I kept my distance from land

and moved northward, always piloting with plenty of water under my keel. Glancing toward shore, I was startled to see a large, white cross in the dark trees. It seemed to shine, and I wondered what it was. I paused momentarily to admire its beauty.

After I completed my voyage, I drove my elderly 4 x 4 vehicle down a winding cliffside road off Hwy. 61 toward Lake Superior. At the bottom rose the white cross.

It was not the original wooden cross. After the cross erected by Father Baraga had fallen because of weather-worn decay, the faithful had constructed a concrete cross that could be seen a long distance from the lake.

Looking around, I wondered how the canoeists made their landing here in a storm. Cold and exhausted, they must have frantically searched for a landing as their canoe was carried atop each wave crest. Ahead lay the rocky shore but no place to pull into with their canoe.

Then they found the mouth of what is now called the Cross River, and their shallow-draft canoe slid over a sandbar to the small stream that ran down the hillside. I noticed that the stream was not discernable from the lake. It is located behind a projection of rocks and trees—a hidden stream. I wondered how they found it.

We sailed out of Keweenaw Bay and past the Huron Islands. On our right rose the Huron Mountains, in all their rugged beauty. I suspected these scenic, wild areas had changed little since the days of Father Baraga and Father Menard.

By 8:15 pm., and with dark shadows settling over the hills, we were inside the breakwaters of Presque Isle Harbor, just north of Marquette. Minutes later, we tied up in the beautiful marina's clear but shallow waters. At a nearby taconite dock, a thousand-foot-long ore boat was being filled.

My thoughts turned once again to Superior's black robes. One died in the wilderness and lay in an unknown and unmarked grave. But in nearby Marquette lie the remains of the Snowshoe Priest. He died in 1868 at 71 and is buried in the crypt of St. Peter's Cathedral, located on Marquette's 4th and Baraga Streets. Once this voyage was over, I would return to pay my respects to these incredible black robes—who were also fellow boaters. ❀

18

Mystery of the Pits

What secrets do the ancient rocks hold?

THE PUKASKWA PITS along the Canadian north shore are among Lake Superior's archeological mysteries. Some historians speculate the pits were used for solitary religious spirit quests or vision searches. Native Americans were believed to fast until a vision revealed mysterious secrets or gave them glimpses into the future.

"Any pits around here?" I asked my Canadian friends.

Reg Essa, the skipper of *Rejoyce,* surprised me. "Near the tip of this island."

Pukaskwa Pits on Thompson Island?

"What do the pits look like?"

"We'll show you," Reg said.

Doug Irwin's inflatable craft glided over the cove's sheltered waters. Soon we ran the boat up on the beach, and Reg and I scrambled ashore. We worked our way up a slight incline, past scattered trees and brush, and emerged into a primeval stillness.

A rocky beach lay ahead with smooth gray stones, some as large as flattened footballs and covered by lichen. The peculiar roundness of the rocks suggested that eons of Superior's wind, rain, and waves had shaped them.

"There they are," Reg said, moving toward a shallow depression ahead of us. He picked his way down into a shallow pit until he stood knee-level. The hole was about three feet deep, dish-shaped, and nine feet long.

I walked around the oval-shaped pit, found a short, rough stairway on the northern side, and walked down to stand beside Reg. At the bottom, I saw more rocks and gravel.

So this was the mysterious pit.

It was, I learned, one of the farthest west of these mysterious depressions. But what was it for?

The religious ceremony explanation came to my mind. I imagined an early inhabitant, an ancestor of the Ojibway, hunkering down in this pit overlooking the big water and waiting for a vision to appear.

I crouched down, looking over the rim. Superior loomed vast and brooding, overpowering at times, with a few whitecaps.

No visions. But then again, I had not starved myself or gone sleepless for days. This was not likely, either.

"One recent theory is that they were used for shelter," Reg said. "Whoever dug them would bring their canoes ashore and pull them over the pits."

I sat down. There was room in my pit for several people, maybe enough for a couple of paddlers from the birchbark canoes that moved along this watery highway so long ago.

I felt a lump. Yes, it was a cobble rock. I turned the other cheek. There was another rock poking at my jeans. The pit would not be the most comfortable place to spend a night or even a weather-bound couple days.

"By getting down in a pit," Reg said, "a man can get out of the wind and get some protection from the elements. These pits occur all along the North Shore."

I could envision pulling my birch-bark canoe up from the water and turning it over the pit. But I foresaw a problem: The canoe would not fit upside down because of its ancient design—the bow and the stern are upturned in classic birch bark canoe fashion.

Some very practical paddlers developed the design a long time ago. The upturned bow would deflect Superior's heavy waves from coming aboard and streamline the canoe from headwinds.

But placed on the pit, if they turned the canoe on its *side*, the small craft would provide a sturdy roof. A cloth draped over the upturned bottom would complete an emergency shelter.

If I were windbound or caught in a rainstorm—or one of Superior's infamous storms—a pit like this might give me an excellent shelter. And quickly.

It would not be the Hilton, but the stones around me would take the brunt of the wind and the weather, and my canoe would be my roof. I'd be out of the wind and rain and resting not-too-uncomfortably on packs or furs.

It seemed to make sense. The pits were shelters. There were a lot of pits along the northern shore, which indicated that they were widely used for paddle-driven craft making a traverse of the lake.

If the weather came up, you just got off the lake. You pulled your canoe on the beach a short distance to a pit and turned it over on its side. Voila! You have shelter.

One of my favorite Canadian authors, Farley Mowat (*Cry Wolf* and *The Farfarers*), tells of staying ashore under an overturned canoe, with a tarpaulin pegged down on the tall side to complete the protection. He wrote that he lived in "a fair comfort and ease while wind-bound."

Another question occurred to me: Why didn't the voyageurs and native travelers drag their canoes and gear into the nearby woods? The pine and fir trees would have taken off the brunt of the wind.

But the canoes carried heavy goods and supplies, so the less distance you had to lug that weight ashore, the better. Also, in the summer, the north woods had a particular menace that drove paddlers mad: the black flies. Hordes of them lived in the deep woods, but strong winds from Superior usually drove them away from the beach where the pits were located.

In the setting sun's golden rays, we left the pits and the tip of Thompson Island. Thanks to my friends, I was able to locate a Pukaskwa Pit, sit in it, and try to figure out for myself what it was used for. I felt a resonance and an admiration for those who preceded me on the Big Lake. They took their comforts where they could find them and were probably glad to have shelter for the night, even if it were only a pit. ✵

19

The Lone Racer

*America's solo racing hero plunges into
his greatest challenge*

COYOTE WAS A BRUTE, the most awesome racer that Mike Plant ever built. His dream was to sail her through everything that the world's oceans could throw at them—and win the Vendee Globe Challenge.

It would be a circumnavigation of nearly 24,000 miles in one of the most demanding sea races ever conceived. There was no crew nor outside help. Only one sailor could drive the racer around the world. Nonstop.

Mike had already sailed through hurricanes, dodged icebergs, fought six-story-high waves, and even survived a capsize in the Indian Ocean. He was America's most accomplished single-handed offshore sailor and, after three daring circumnavigations, Mike was now ready to start a fourth with his bold new sailboat.

This time, in the world's toughest sailboat race.

The office telephone rang. "Hello, my name is Mike Plant," the voice politely began, "We met when you were doing a story on Outward Bound."

Yes, I remembered: a youngish guy, whip-thin, with a deep tan and sun-blasted hair—definitely an outdoor type. He was teaching survival and team-building through Wilderness Adventures.

Mike grew up on the shores of Minnesota's Lake Minnetonka, on the western edge of Minneapolis. By age twelve, he was winning sailboat races.

He was a "doer," his mother Mary Plant recalled, "The spirit of adventure came as he got older. He was full of action."

But he also had a problem. When Mike was two years old, his mother saw him hold various items close to his eyes to examine them. She took her young son to have his eyes checked.

"As it turned out, he was very nearsighted," Mary told me. "He started to wear thick glasses and was later designated legally blind." In his early teens, he wore contact lenses.

Despite his handicap, he made a name for himself as an adventurer and a survival specialist. He once hiked from his home in Minnesota through South America to the end of land at Tierra del Fuego. Mike traveled 12,000 miles through remote provinces and dangerous jungles—and could have been easy prey for bandits and mercenaries.

"How'd you do that?" I asked.

"I didn't have anything they wanted," he answered.

Mike took naturally to Outward Bound. During World War II, the organization was conceived in Great Britain when many British seamen unaccountably died at sea while awaiting rescue after being torpedoed by German U-Boats. The program was designed to instill self-reliance, spiritual tenacity, and develop innate abilities to help seamen survive under challenging conditions.

He bought a used thirty-foot Cheoy Lee sailboat at Bayfield, Wisconsin, near the Apostle Islands, and, after fixing it up, sailed eastward across Superior. He crossed the Great Lakes to New York and then sailed the North Atlantic to St. Thomas in the Virgin Islands. Mike lived on his boat in the islands and worked when he could as a carpenter.

When spring came, he sailed northward with a friend, but neither knew where they wanted to go. His friend suggested they go to Newport to observe the start of the Newport-to-Bermuda sailboat race. While there, Mike worked as a charter skipper to deliver other boats to ports in the US and the Caribbean. Between assignments, he earned money doing carpentry and house painting.

In 1983, he saw a film about an around-the-world sailboat race. "It changed my life," he told me. The 1982-83 BOC Challenge was a yacht race for around-the-world solo sailors. Suddenly, Mike knew what he wanted to be: a long-distance solo sailboat racer.

He told me: "When I walked out of the theater, it was like a light switch had gone on. I've never really looked back."

But it was a long way between dreaming about being an ocean racer and getting a seaworthy boat to enter a race. The nautical competition was fierce. The well-funded European syndicates dominated the around-the-world sailboat races, especially those backing the French racing superstars.

Their boats and their skippers seemed unbeatable.

Undeterred, Mike told his mother: "I'm going in the next race."

His answer to the high cost of racing was building his boat himself. He worked evenings and weekends on a shoestring budget in his front yard while working days as a building contractor. Friends pitched in to help him on his fifty-foot water-ballasted sloop, working from a new design by Rodger Martin. Mike was the naval architect's first customer.

Somehow, Mike hoped to compete against the world's top racers with their multi-million-dollar designs and well-honed racing organization with his home-built boat.

He took his racer to the BOC Challenge starting line in Newport in 1986. In this around-the-world competition, solo sailors raced their sailboats 27,550 miles around the world, with only three stops.

As he set off in *Airco Distributor,* all three of his autopilots failed, one by one. He would have to hand-steer to the next stop.

"I'm not going to turn back," he radioed.

Mike's home-built boat circled the globe in a total time of 157 days, 11 hours, and 44 minutes. He bettered the previous record by fifty days.

The international racing world took notice. A lone American had become one of the world's most successful single-handed offshore sailors.

Around the old sailing port of Newport, Mike was no longer another boat bum and dreamer. He was a proven fire-in-the-belly skipper—a real racer.

And he had only begun.

Mike Plant resplendent in a tall hat on the *Duracell.*

Photo/ Billy Black

In 1989, extreme sailboat racers conceived The Vendee Globe Challenge as nothing less than the ultimate ocean racer's race.

It was a race around the world, all alone, without stops for rest or reprovisioning. Racers would not be able to get outside help. The brutal, nonstop marathon would run 24,000 miles, west to east, rounding the earth's most dreaded capes, including the fearsome Cape Horn and the misnamed Cape of Good Hope. A sailor would not only have to fight through survival conditions but do so while carrying as much sail as he could as long as he could.

This was the ultimate race and represented a tremendous new challenge.

It also meant a new boat. Again, Mike turned to his friend Rodger Martin for a design to speed him around the world nonstop.

Unable to get enough sponsors to fund his new racing challenge, Mike dug deeply into his meager resources to build his boat. He began construction of his sixty-foot boat in a rented shed. *Duracell* would have twin rudders, a super-fast hull, and state-of-the-art water ballast. Mike sailed the boat across the North Atlantic to France to qualify for the race.

After the race began, he became the early leader, despite suffering from a virus infection for a week. He toughed it out and got well at sea while he raced.

In the Pacific Ocean, disaster struck: a five-dollar part broke on the rigging. Mike sailed thirty-six hours straight until he could anchor off Campbell Island, New Zealand. A storm caught him and began pushing the sailboat toward a rocky shore.

Four meteorologists saw the racer's plight and motored out in their Zodiac. Mike had to accept the tow to save his boat with its dragging anchor, but he knew the outside assistance would disqualify him.

The meteorologists suggested that he continue the race, and they vowed eternal silence. No one would know.

"Except I would," Mike answered.

Mike radioed the race committee that he had accepted outside help but would continue the race, though disqualified. He unofficially crossed the finish line in seventh place.

Mike lost the race, but to the admiring French, he emerged a hero. The Minnesotan's determination and honesty did not go unnoticed: 25,000 people lined the breakwater in Les Sables-d'Olonne to give him a hero's welcome.

Mike was the only American in the race. Herb McCormick, the editor of *Cruising World* and the Boating Editor of the *New York Times*, wrote: "The tens of thousands of French men and women who greeted him at the finish understood something that was largely missed in this country. By forging on, by completing what he'd set out to do, by showing the highest respect for his competitors in a wonderful act of sportsmanship, Mike was as much a winner as the sailors who'd officially cross the finish line."

Despite his delays, Mike set the American record to circumnavigate single-handed for the shortest time. He did it in 134 days.

In 1990 he upgraded and modified *Duracell* to enter the BOC Challenge, again setting sail from Newport. His effort caught the eye of Minnesota Senator David Durenberger, who read a section of a *New York Times* report into the *Congressional Record.* He noted that Mike was the only American in the single-handed, around-the-world nonstop yacht race that sailors regarded as "the ultimate test of courage, stamina, and resourcefulness."

As *Duracell* neared Cape Town, South Africa, in the 6,800-mile first leg of the race, Senator Durenberger read into the *Record:*

> *After thirty-five days on the open seas, fatigue has become*
> *Mike's constant companion. Mike has slept in his bunk only*
> *twice during the trip. His daily sleeping routine is to work*
> *and sleep in twenty-minute intervals. Hundreds of miles*
> *from the nearest shore, Mike is now running low on food.*
> *Most of his remaining food supply exists in the form of*

carbohydrates and starches, namely beans and rice. But Mike and the **Duracell** *are likely to overcome their obstacles and regain lost ground during the next two legs of the race. It is in these two legs that the winds above the southern seas are stronger than in any other part of the race. As Mike traverses through the turbulent seas below the equator, the spirit of Minnesota will go with him.*

"Mike thrives on the interrelationship with nature that solo offshore sailboat racing provides. He once said that offshore sailboat racing 'strips you to the soul—exposing who we are, what we are, (and) why we exist.' To Minnesotans and Americans alike, Mike's courage, leadership, and ability to overcome adversity symbolize who we are, what we are, and why we exist. His spirit of competition and determination serves as a beacon of goodwill from Minnesota to the world.

In Cape Town, South Africa, a competitor collided with his boat. Mike somehow repaired his racer while he continued to race. He made it around the world in 132 days and 20 hours, bettering his previous time by two days—setting a new US record for solo circumnavigation.

He was now America's premiere single-handed sailor. In only six years, he had come out of nowhere to stand on the threshold of greatness and fame. In France, he got the nickname "Top Gun" because of his passion for carrying sail in heavy seas and wild winds.

A certain mystique surrounded him. He had savvy, capability, and endurance. He came to love the solitude and the challenge of single-handed, long-distance racing. He was happiest when he was alone at sea with his boat. When family and sailing friends didn't hear from him, they knew it was because he was into "his racing mode." They'd hear from him when the race was over.

He was passionate about his boat, his race, and his dream.

Mike on the busy foredeck of *Coyote*. It takes a lot of energy to raise a 250-pound sail up an 85-foot mast.

Photo/ Billy Black

The challenge was getting harder. To compete in the 1992-93 Vendee Globe Challenge, Mike would need as powerful a boat as he could get to keep up with the aggressive and better-funded French racers. The vessel had to be strong, light, and above all, it had to be fast.

Once again, he turned to Rodger Martin to design a breakthrough boat. Mike knew what he wanted, and he had more than a handful of ideas.

Another around-the-world sailor, Dodge Morgan, who was the first American to sail alone nonstop around the world, had an ominous viewpoint: "Mike had a boat designed close to the edge and built perhaps a little closer."

He added, "Mike knew what he was doing, and so did the people who worked with him. They wanted to win a race."

Coyote was a boat ahead of its time, a flat-out super boat, a high-performance ocean dragster powered by a vast sail area, and a knife-blade keel. It was designed to do only one thing: rip around the world at top speed and win the Vendee Globe Race.

Coyote was a skimmer at sixty feet in length that could soar over the waves rather than plow through them. She projected brute force with a menacing plumb bow, flat transom, and a straight sheer line.

"Beautiful, but with a raw, brutal type of beauty," *Coyote's* sailmaker, Dan Neri, described her.

"That thing is an animal," one sailor said. "That boat could be difficult to handle with a crew of ten on board."

She was beamy at nearly nineteen feet four inches in width and flat on the deck, like an "aircraft carrier," as her naval architect sometimes joked. She had a low freeboard, which gave her little wind resistance but made her a wet boat. She could catch and fling back waves she couldn't fly over.

Incredibly, *Coyote's* sixty-foot hull itself only drew one foot, one inch of water.

Inside, you had to squat to move around: she only had four feet of headroom, except in the small doghouse, which had headroom of six feet.

Mike was a fanatic on lightness since less weight to drag around equated to a faster boat. *Coyote* was a solid but ultra-lightweight flyer with her E-glass set in epoxy over a foam-core construction. She would displace only 21,500 pounds, nearly 6,000 pounds lighter than his *Duracell.*

Like most of her class of ocean racers, she had a long foretriangle with her mast set back at more than fifty percent of the waterline so she could carry an effective inner forestay.

Dan Neri explained: "It is not practical to change headsails with one man on a boat that big, so they use a reaching/light-wind headsail on the forward stay and a heavy air jib on the inner stay."

Both foresails were set on furlers, with controls leading back to the cockpit.

The big boat would set about fifty percent more sail area than *Duracell,* a small cloud of 2,935 square feet.

Coyote's mainsail alone was 1,630 square feet and weighed 250 pounds. To raise the mainsail from the boom to the top of the mast would take Mike about ten minutes of hard work on a winch. Her largest spinnaker was 2,800 square feet.

Her eighty-five-foot-high mast was built of braided carbon fiber and glass and was light at about three pounds per foot. With its advanced triple-spreader design, it was thin and flexible. That meant the mast would need attention to keep it tuned and in a column.

But *Coyote* would be fast.

Coyote had a fourteen-foot deep "knife blade" keel for minimum resistance while ripping through the world's oceans. The length of the keel's blade from front to back was forty inches and only six inches in thickness.

Constructed of 42 Kevlar and carbon fiber layers, the keel encapsulated a stainless steel plate at its bottom. Six stainless steel bolts extended through the plate and the bulb. The whole unit was overlapped with fifteen carbon fiber layers for extra strength.

The torpedo-shaped lead bulb weighed 8,400 pounds and was 112 inches long, 18 inches high, and 27 inches wide.

Coyote used an extra 7,000 pounds of transferable water ballast in two tanks to get extra weight in her windward side for a wild reach.

For safety, she had five airtight compartments for floatation. With her Airex foam core hull, she had enough floatation to remain afloat even if she was holed and her hull flooded with water.

Mike's *Coyote* was the most extreme sixty-foot monohull ever launched in the U.S. It would be the ultimate weapon to race nonstop around the world.

"She was the fastest, wildest, wettest monohull that I have ever sailed," wrote Herb McCormick.

When I met him again at the Minneapolis Boat Show, Mike was having financial problems. He told me that funds for his new boat were very slow in coming in. He hoped to rely on sponsors and other financial help to get his boat built. Racers like *Coyote* could cost $650,000 to $800,000, and sometimes more—a lot more. It depended on what exotic materials you wanted to put into them.

To win races, he couldn't scrimp. He needed the exotics.

Mike talked about doing a book with me, but that project faded when I regretfully pointed out the time required to research, write, and publish a manuscript: years. Mike didn't have the time.

Mike faced many construction details on his racer built at Concordia Custom Yachts of South Dartmouth, Massachusetts. He was not a sailor to order with a boatyard and then show up when the boat was ready. It was his racer, and from his extensive racing experience, he had specific things in mind.

"Mike knew what he wanted, and he had a great understanding of what the boat would be put through," Dan Neri explained.

Dan had been with Mike when the boat was being built. "Mike was deeply involved in the decision-making for the assembly of the structural parts of the boat," he said. "Some of these decisions were made on the fly, to the point where Mike was drawing on scraps of plywood to illustrate his ideas."

The boat was in a "slow build" program: the yard started it and built it, on and off, as Mike came up with the money.

"Mike was a hands-on man in everything he did," Dan said. "He was trying to manage the boat build, mast engineering and construction, sail inventory planning, electronics installation, fundraising, and preparations for sea trials, and ultimately, his campaign for the Vendee Globe. He had a charisma that drew people to his cause, and a small army of people in Rhode Island did what we could to help him out. I am sure many of us have thought we should have pulled him aside and tried to talk him into slowing down."

But that was not to be. "With Mike, there was no indecision," Dan said. "Everything was about meeting the next goal."

Coyote was intended to be a high-tech, custom-built dreamboat racer using the best of everything new.

"Dan added: "In some areas, the design was beyond the experience base."

"The team at Concordia was among the best in the business. If any group could pull off this build project, it was these guys, and at the time, a seat-of-the-pants approach to high-tech yacht building was not so unusual. But looking back on it, we were pushing too close to the limits of the materials."

Instead of an early 1992 launch, followed by leisurely sea trials in fair weather on the North Atlantic, the boat came off the ramps September 10—six months behind Mike's original schedule.

The critical keel-to-bulb assembly was completed only days before the launch date.

Mike had only seven weeks to get the boat ready and be in France for the race.

Coyote's power was phenomenal. She accelerated quickly, and on a reach, she tore across the water, nothing like a boat Mike had ever sailed. Her cruising speed was calculated at fifteen knots.

Dan Neri pointed out: "There are considerations for handling an extreme boat like this. At sixty feet in length, *Coyote* was a sailing dinghy. You plan about four steps but focus on the next step at all times."

Coyote had no engine. A powerboat, usually an inflatable, towed the big boat to get in and out of the harbor during sea trials. Getting her underway was complicated because her mast was far aft.

"The boat wanted to sail backward with just the mainsail up." For that reason, "it was important to keep it going forward at all times."

With Dan aboard, Mike tested *Coyote* off Newport in Rhode Island Sound.

"My most vivid memories are of looking up the rig while reaching in 25 knots of wind and the boat crashing along at 11 knots. The mast lacked torsional stiffness for some reason. Either the tube did not have enough off-axis wraps, the spreader geometry was wrong, or it did not have enough shroud tension.

"The mast moved more than any rig I had seen before or since. The mast was built in four sections, joined at the boat shop. Mike had a set of alloy spreaders that I think were supposed to be used for the mold to make carbon spreaders, but they were used on the mast instead. So it was a big, high-load spar system, built by a group of excellent composite boat builders, but without the benefit of the level of engineering we are accustomed to today."

Coyote was "incredibly loud inside" when sailing with the breeze forward of the beam. "It was also very loud off the wind, but the off-the-wind noises were not as alarming. Today, we are used to the noise, but with *Coyote* being the first of its type, the noise was new and a little unnerving."

"The best day of sailing was during a photoshoot off the mouth of the Sakonnet River. There were long ocean swells from a low-pressure system well offshore and a twenty-knot sea breeze.

"We had the kite up, surfing in the high teens, and all of the crew were inside the boat so that the helicopter could film Mike sailing it alone. Davis Murray, Mike's buddy from the Virgin Islands, was steering with the autopilot while looking out the windows.

"As a joke, Davis made the boat bear off at the bottom of a trough while Mike was standing on the bow in the hero pose, with one hand on the head stay. The bow dug in, and the wave caromed back along the foredeck. When the water cleared, Mike was standing there, drenched, and smiling.

"We did it again. This time, Mike held on to the headstay with both hands and let the wave pick him up so that his whole body was streaming aft, parallel with the deck."

Crew high jinks aside, *Coyote* was proving to be a remarkable boat. "Compared to a heavy displacement boat, I would say that *Coyote* felt like she was on rails most of the time. The boat was very fast, and you get directional stability with speed. The flip side is that if the autopilot wanders too far, a fast boat can take a quick turn toward the wind. Steering problems are usually a function of the sail trim and pilot setup rather than boat design."

Mike discovered a few problems. As Dan relates: "*Coyote* did not go to weather as well as a typical fully crewed race boat. Her hull shape is optimized for reaching and running. In a long-distance ocean race, the only times you want to be hard on the wind is when you leave harbors and approach harbors. Otherwise, you sail a slightly more freed-up angle toward a more favorable part of the weather system."

Mary Plant minced no words. When going to weather, she said, "Of all the boats Mike had, *Coyote* was the most miserable."

During sea trials, Mike discovered that when *Coyote* reached a speed of about nine knots, the keel's foil and bulb began emitting a humming sound. The crew checked out the keel through a sight glass—a piece of Plexiglas built into the hull to observe the keel while underway. But they could not see any problem.

In addition to the noise, they felt a vibration coming from the keel. As *Coyote's* speed increased, the sound and the vibrations would change. Mike dismissed the noise and vibrations as problems common to racers like *Coyote.*

Overall, Mike was happy. His new racer performed brilliantly, and he worked hard to learn her unique ways. But the harder he worked, the further he seemed to fall behind.

Mike was a list keeper. He said that he had a million things left to do before he left. He confided to a friend that his list now was "so long I've lost the beginning of it."

Sailing to Annapolis, *Coyote* continued to reveal her potential. Spreading her wings on the North Atlantic, the racer averaged sixteen knots, and during one stretch, she reached a sustained speed of twenty-four knots. Mike was delighted.

But in the Chesapeake Bay, *Coyote* ran into trouble. Under sail at 9:30 a.m., *Coyote* was east of the entrance of Annapolis harbor on a reach and hitting upwards of nine knots with a jib up and a reef in her main.

"These were perfect conditions for what Mike had in mind," photographer Billy Black said. "Flat water, good wind."

Billy was at the wheel when *Coyote's* deep keel abruptly plowed into the bottom. A soft thud echoed through the hull. The bow did a slight dip, and she slid to a stop. "It was a soft, gentle landing," Billy recalls. "We just settled in."

She had buried her fourteen-foot-deep bulb into the bottom mud. *Coyote* started to cant sideways in the twelve-knot wind out of the north, tugging at her keel.

Mike tried to sail her off. He succeeded in heeling the sailboat over and turned her about 180 degrees. But this did not dislodge the ballast bulb from the mud. She remained stuck.

Coyote sails past the Statue of Liberty to begin her crossing of the North Atlantic.

Photo/ Billy Black

A twenty-foot fishing boat passed by. Mike hailed it for help and passed *Coyote's* halyard to the powerboat for more leverage to get the bulb out of the mud. The obliging skipper gave the throttle some gas, and *Coyote's* mast top took up the strain. But the bulb remained stuck.

Time for another try. Mike passed a towing line aft of the bow and another line to the stern. The powerboat throttled up and slowly, *Coyote's* long hull canted sideways—and the buried bulb popped loose.

Back at the dock in Annapolis, Mike and his crew took turns looking down the sight glass at the keel. No one noticed anything abnormal.

"Mike took it in stride," Billy said. "No problems."

Later, as they sailed out of Annapolis, *Coyote* again went aground in the bay. This time, two workboats took the sailboat in tow and yanked her off the bottom.

Mike wondered if he should take *Coyote* to a boatyard, hoist her out of the water, and personally inspect for damage. The two groundings could have damaged the keel and the fasteners that held the ballast bulb.

But there was no time.

The North Atlantic—and the big race—lay ahead.

In New York harbor, *Coyote* made a triumphant debut. She looked sleek and able, a beautiful young racer eager to do battle with the dark waters of the world.

With Mike at the helm, *Coyote* slipped along, quick to respond even under the reduced sail of a reefed main and a small jib. Just a little sail was enough to move the boat smartly.

The schedule was tight, but Mike planned to sail out of New York on Friday, October 16, and arrive October 30 in Les Sables-d'Olonne, France, 3,200 miles away. A two-week sailboat passage across the North Atlantic would be swift, but *Coyote* was a fast boat, and Mike had been across "the Big Pond" many times. He knew how to drive his boat hard if he needed to.

Departure day was sunny but ominously breezy, with a strong wind out of the southeast. Well-wishers stopped by to bid Mike a swift voyage, including famed America's Cup sailor Dennis Conner, who walked over to give Mike a copy of his latest book.

"Maybe this will help you," Dennis joked. Mike enjoyed a good laugh: Dennis' new book was about how to sail.

Al Roker from NBC's "Today Show" interviewed Mike. Millions of viewers saw the young Minnesota sailor about to depart on his globe-girdling quest in his new racer. The TV show planned a satellite broadcast with Mike during the race.

Under a powerboat's tow, *Coyote* gracefully moved into the harbor and past the historic windjammers at the South Street Seaport Museum. Mike cast off *Coyote's* towline and raised the sails.

The big racer came to life. In the rising southeast wind, a cloud of canvas tightened, then grew taut as the boat heeled and gracefully moved out of the harbor, eager for its first crossing.

As Mike and *Coyote* loped off into the distance and the awaiting North Atlantic, watchers stood in awe.

"He looked straight ahead," a spectator said. "He never looked back."

Late in the season, the North Atlantic was changing. Always potentially dangerous, the ocean could quickly turn into a nightmare of gale-force winds, bitter cold, and broken seas as winter came on.

By the third day, the wind was blowing on the bow at 35 knots, and Mike was having trouble steering in heavy seas.

In a radio message to a friend, he referred to the storm as "god-awful."

As a veteran of numerous North Atlantic crossings, he expected to encounter rough conditions. But he did not anticipate the stomach-churning jolts and crashes as his extreme racer speared waves and scooped water back over the deck.

He was in the Gulf Stream, where the Labrador Current becomes a virtual river of water running toward the east—a potential lift of several knots toward France. But the storm was out of the east, and winds were blowing against the fast-moving stream, piling it into giant haystacks of waves.

Coyote would fly down the backside of one wave and bury her bow in the oncoming wave. Her bow would yank up; she'd fling back a fire-hose spray before she'd climb over the wave.

It was a brutal, abrupt motion, punishing to boat and man.

Mike had trouble steering in the heavy seas, struggling to hold *Coyote's* bow close to the wind.

Coyote's worst point of sail was going upwind: she was designed to be a downwind flyer. She pounded into the waves with her relatively flat bottom, razor keel, and extreme light displacement. It all added up to a bruising, miserable ride.

Mike managed his sail plan by deeply reefing the main and hanking on a storm jib on the inner forestay—a patch of sail.

He braced himself behind the wheel, trying to summon all his reserves of strength and energy.

His deadline loomed.

On October 21, about a third of the way across the Atlantic and 940 miles from New York, he saw the freighter, SKS *Trader.* He used his hand-held VHF radio to report to the captain: "I have no power, but I'm working on the problem."

He had lost not only his radios but all of his electrical power.

Without his electrical systems, he could no longer operate his autopilots. That meant he had to hand-steer.

Mike had to watch her carefully, for she was just too slippery a racer to let fly along unattended. In these stormy conditions, he couldn't lash the wheel and go below for a decent night's sleep. He tried catnapping at the wheel.

Belowdecks, the racer was a maze of vibrations and movement as she sliced through the water. Her hull was alive with the noises of her passage; she boomed when she fell off a wave. The keel made a loud humming noise and vibrated at above nine knots. *Coyote* picked up speed when she raced down a wave's back, which made the shaking and the clatter get worse.

There was little comfort belowdecks, anyway, since *Coyote* was stripped out for speed. The boat's interior was outfitted with a minimum of amenities and equipment: a chart table with computers and navigational equipment, some shelves, and a stove to heat food. There were stacks of food and provisions everywhere.

He'd have time to sort things out in France after he met his deadline.

The electrical system had worked OK during the brief shakedown to Annapolis but had failed miserably at sea. *Coyote* had two electrical systems: a 12-volt and also a 24-volt. In theory, the 24-volt system would run his autopilots better and faster, a significant advantage for a fast-moving ocean greyhound. But it also meant that Mike had to deal with dual-voltage systems and the related gear to power them, including generators, relays, regulators, and wiring.

Whatever the problem was, *Coyote's* power was out. Mike was in trouble.

By Friday, October 30, Mike had not arrived at the docks in Les Sables-d'Olonne, France. He had been out of touch since October 21.

In France, Mike's crew contacted the French Coast Guard to initiate a search. But they were turned down, with the explanation that the French Coast Guard needed a formal request from the U.S. Coast Guard. Mike's parents, Mary and Frank Plant, requested a search for their missing son. The U.S. Coast Guard declined because they had insufficient information about where to search.

On Friday, November 13, the U.S. Coast Guard issued an alert for all passing ships to be on the lookout for the missing racer. They began a search covering an area northwest of Bermuda, on coordinates supplied by Canadian Mission Control. The coordinates were hundreds of miles south of Mike's intended course. On November 18, the search was revised to include an area north of the Azores. The searchers found nothing.

A day later, the search was called off.

In the meantime, a volunteer group, the Friends of Mike Plant, began lobbying their senators, members of Congress, and other elected officials to press for an additional search for the missing sailor. I was a member of that group.

The Navy authorized two P-3 Orion planes to join the search with infrared sensors that could detect heat in the water. The aircraft flew out of New Brunswick Naval Air Station in Maine. They joined four Coast Guard C-130 search planes from North Carolina and Florida.

Meteorologists and navigation experts attempted to determine Mike's probable location based on wind, speed, and weather conditions. They pinpointed an area well east of the original search area, north of the Azores.

On November 20, the Coast Guard resumed its search of an area north of the Azores. Aircraft and ships from four nations looked in an area that eventually covered more than 215,000 square miles of open ocean.

It was one of the broadest rescue missions ever in the North Atlantic and eventually involved aircraft and vessels from the U.S. Coast Guard, U.S. Navy, Canada, Great Britain, and France.

But they found nothing.

On Sunday morning, November 22, the 750-foot Greek tanker, *Protank Orinocco,* saw something dark lying low in the water, drifting upside down. Its bottom was awash in eight to twelve-foot waves.

The hull appeared intact, with twin rudders still upright and a tall keel fin pointed heavenward. But part of the vessel's keel, the ballast bulb, was missing.

In heavy seas and rain, the tanker came within fifty feet and cautiously circled the upside-down hull, scanning the boat with binoculars, searching for any signs of life. They saw none.

Because of sea conditions, the tanker could not send a boat to board the upturned hull, but they recorded her position. They found the lost vessel 1,100 nautical miles due west of Les Sables-d'Olonne, France, and 500 nautical miles north of the Azores.

They waited. Even in heavy seas, they knew that the sound of the tanker's big engines and thrashing propeller alongside the hull would throb loudly through the water, alerting anyone inside.

No one appeared from the overturned hull nor gave any signal.

Later that day, two Coast Guard C-130s, a Navy P-3 Orion, and a French Navy patrol craft searched near the sightings. A British aircraft flew over the lost boat and conducted a flare search in the vicinity of the hull. They could find nothing in the water, such as a life raft or wreckage.

Still, hope remained. Sailors worldwide felt that Mike had a fighting chance of being rescued if he went aboard his life raft or survived inside the upturned hull, which was riding high in the water. Other racers had lived for days inside their overturned but intact hulls.

Three days later, the French tugboat, *Malabar,* arrived alongside the overturned sailboat and positively identified the hull as the missing racer, *Coyote.*

French frogmen dove under the vessel and came up inside the hull, shining their lights about as they searched through the watertight compartments. They found air pockets inside where a man could breathe.

They located the life raft opened in the cockpit but uninflated. The CO_2 bottle had not been fired. A survival bag was attached to the raft. Nearby lay an unopened bag of distress flares. They found a life jacket tied to a bunk, and they also saw the partial remains of a torn survival suit.

But there were no signs of the missing sailor.

The searchers concluded that the lone sailor was no longer alive because they had found the life raft and survival gear, but no one aboard the overturned hull.

They left. *Coyote* remained capsized and adrift at sea.

I called the Minnesota governor's office. As a member of the Mike Plant Committee, I had requested the governor's office involve itself in implementing the search for the lost Minnesotan.

But now I could only relay the message I got from the French frogmen: They had found the life raft, but no one aboard and that, in their words, "there are no other possibilities."

In the fading light of a late November afternoon, I drove to Lake Minnetonka's old Lafayette Club near the beloved waters that Mike had sailed as a boy. People from around the world were gathered for a memorial service to celebrate Mike's life. We shared our memories of him and his thoughts, words, and passions.

Mark Schrader, a fellow long-distance ocean racer, admired Mike's calm professionalism, saying with admiration, "He sailed the world as though he were sailing across the lake."

Rodger Martin, *Coyote's* designer, talked about Mike's remarkable concentration. The tall naval architect recalled driving by the boatyard when it was closed for a winter holiday. He saw Mike, all alone, working the boatyard's travel lift in the icy yard, slowly lowering his boat onto its awaiting keel. Surprised by the visitor, Mike turned—and fell. He had been concentrating so intently that his boat shoes had frozen to the ground.

One sailor told us he'd once asked Mike why he didn't feel fear when he raced a sailboat around the world. "It's too exciting," Mike had replied.

Most of us shared a sailor's sense of comradeship. Mike's ordeal on the North Atlantic was over. We would not see him again, but we knew he had left us doing what he wanted to do. It was a sailor's ending.

Those who had been privileged to spend time with Mike had our lives enriched. We admired his quiet courage, and we were astonished by his prodigious deeds.

Many of us could not fully comprehend that the North Atlantic had finally claimed him. He was our hero.

It was night when I drove out of the parking lot. My headlights shone over the dark lake that lapped at the shore. The trees were bare, their thin branches swaying in the chill north wind.

This was the lake that Mike sailed as a boy. He had gone on to do incredible things, and, somehow, thoughts of Mike's final moments kept coming alive in my mind. My mind turned to the North Atlantic.

It was after midnight, and the seas were rough. Black waves reared toward him. Mike was at the helm, shivering in the dark beside his big wheel. He was probably telling himself that his boat could make it if they'd just hang in there.

Coyote clawed into the wind; sails sheeted nearly flat. Slamming into the oncoming waves, *Coyote's* long hull quivered with each shock. The lone skipper must have felt every blow in his tired, bruised body.

Deep below the hull, the 8,400-pound keel bulb's noise and vibrations were worse than ever.

Mike did not slow his racer: he had water ballast in the port ballast tank to help stabilize the boat on its port tack, and he continued heading off at speed.

Mike might have heard final warnings that something was fatally wrong—if there had not been so much noise in the storm. He was in the middle of the North Atlantic—his safety and refuge lay dead ahead—and he had to keep the faith that his boat would hold together. Mike had fought against the odds before, and he had won.

Suddenly, the hull slammed under his feet.

From somewhere below, there was a final cracking, shattering noise.

The damaged carbon fiber holding the bulb plate had finally worn through and broken. The ballast bulb, the keel bolts, and the stainless steel plate dropped off the base.

Coyote bounced up when the ballast weight snapped off. She veered off course, and dark water began marching up her leeward side. Under the pressure of the wind and the oncoming waves, the hull slowly reared up on her beam ends.

She probably hung there for a moment, then went over, hard. Her long boom caught in the water, swung back viciously toward the cockpit, then cracked under pressure. All that remained of the boom was the first two feet attached to the base of the mast.

The tip of her eighty-five-foot mast speared into the water. It began to bend and finally snapped several feet above the deck. The mast slammed back against the cockpit, crushing the top of the cabin doghouse. The broken mast trailed below the overturned hull, held by the stainless-steel rigging.

Coyote came to rest upside down, eerily quiet. Her battle with the North Atlantic was over. ☀

20

Agate Island

Want to go on a treasure hunt?

"WE'RE OFF TO AGATE ISLAND," Lynda Blanchette cheerfully hollered. "Want to come?"

"Sure," I said after a thoughtful pause. It was *their* boat.

Maybe my answer was a little cautious, but I had my reasons.

Agate Island lies east of CPR Harbor, not far from Mystery Island and the Island of Doom. I found out the hard way that the area is rife with reefs.

Searching for the harbor's entryway, I watched *Persistence's* depth sounder, and suddenly, there was a hollow bump noise, a scraping sound; the tiller twitched in my hand. The impact shoved me against the boom.

I looked down into the clear water, and yes, there were rocks below—a lot of them. I was aground.

Worse, I was bumping away on a lee shore with the wind blowing me further onto the reefs. What would happen to *Persistence's* wood hull?

Hastily, I checked to see if I could use my outboard, but I saw that the prop would smash on the rocks if I turned on the engine. I swung the prop up and out of the water. I did not want to be on the rocks without an engine.

I tried kedging with my Danforth anchors, but their flukes only glanced against the rocks, and they came skipping back to me. They would not set. I could not pull *Persistence* off the rocks.

I was running out of options to get her off—until I made a desperate VHF call for help. Lynda answered, and soon I saw a 16-foot aluminum runabout dashing around a bend in the island.

Greg Richard and Jake Hayton pulled me off the reefs and guided me into the small harbor. They were from the *Ogima,* a sturdy 40-foot steel motor cruiser.

Today, they invited me aboard their runabout to visit a curiously named island.

Soon we were zipping out of CPR harbor and onto the lake. I glanced to starboard and saw flagged markers for several reefs I had not noticed earlier. The reef markers were simply hanks of cloth attached to a bendy pole and sticking out of the water maybe 6 feet.

This area was not the easiest to get in and out of unless you knew what you were doing. But Lynda and the crew did. In the shallow-draft runabout, we could skim the surface with no problems.

I had to ask: "Are there agates?"

Lynda grinned. "Why do you think they call it Agate Island?"

It sounded like a great adventure. A unique island of agates on the incredible mineral-rich north shore of Superior. A treasure hunt?

Gregg ran the aluminum runabout on the gravel beach and hopped on the island's western shore. Lynda and Gregg showed me how to look for agates along the beach.

But I could not find one.

"Here," she said, holding up a lovely small rock with a purple part. "An agate."

How had I missed it?

Something poked me through the soles of my beat-up boat moccasins. I bent closer to the beach.

There! I found something and washed it off. It was a lovely little agate.

Hooray for my side. This adventure was like a child's scavenger hunt, with the reward being agates that you found yourself. And kept.

I was not as good as Lynda, who gave me several of her treasures. It was a wonderful time.

On the island, the sun burned down, accompanied by a light breeze. The heaviness in the air made the heat more intense than usual.

The wind had come up while we were agate hunting, and soon, we were back on board the runabout. It was a choppy ride back that splashed foam on me.

It was amazing how quickly the wind had changed. In the stiff breeze, the flags on the reef markers were standing sideways, and the staffs holding them up were bending like willow branches in the wind.

"Getting back just in time," Lynda observed.

I heartily agreed. With a few agates in my pocket, I wasn't wealthy, but it had been a happy time. Lynda smiled. I smiled back. ❀

21

The Northwoods Boatbuilder

What do you want in a boat? Here's some down-home wisdom

THE BINGHAM BOAT WORKS goes back three generations to a grandfather who had a boatyard in Long Island, New York, but moved away from the east coast for his health. He picked Michigan's Upper Peninsula because it had water and clean, fresh air. He initially worked in lumber camps but returned to boat building after regaining his health.

The present boatyard began building and repairing boats in 1930, and they were still building wooden boats when Joe Bingham began working in the family business. "I was born here," he told me. "I'm 53, and you could say that I have been in the boat business all my years."

The Bingham Boat Works is still a family business. Joe's wife does paperwork for the boatworks; a son works full time, and a daughter does upholstery. Another son and daughter-in-law also work part-time. Joe and his wife have eleven children.

"You must have a sense of humor and a thick skin to be in the boat business," he explained. "Not all boat owners are pleasant people. We deal with them all. They are like they are. Most of our business is repeat customers, and they bring us more customers. Word of mouth is precious. We have to work hard, and they know they get a good job here."

Joe was a middle-sized man with big boatbuilder's hands and a down-home wit.

"I only work half days," Joe solemnly explained.

I must have looked surprised, for he added: "Eight to eight, always 12 hours—that's only half a day. It's a part-time job."

Heh. Heh. As we walked through his boatyard, I saw several hulls being built. I clambered up a ladder to get into a recently completed hull. This was one of two hulls under construction; a third one was out in the yard. It stood upright on its keel, with its interior open and ready for finishing off. I was impressed with its no-nonsense, sea-kindly appearance.

A sweet sweep to the sheer ended in a short bowsprit, where an outer jib could be set to produce extra horsepower. The beam was 8 feet 6 inches, and the draft was a minimal 3 feet 11 inches. This was a design for a cruiser, not a racer.

In an era of boat-building superlatives, Joe referred to his craft not as a 28-or-30-footer but simply as a 27.8. "That's the actual length on deck," he said, "leaving off the length of the bowsprit."

The boat was designed to fit in a 30-foot slip, and Joe explained that in some marinas, for a boat longer than 30 feet, you have to rent or buy slips for 40-footers. "That gets expensive."

Joe considers the 27.8 "the maxi trailerable boat," pushing 7,400 pounds.

"If it weighs more than 8,000 pounds, you need a two-ton truck to pull it around."

It is a semi-custom boat, meaning that the boatyard customizes parts of the vessel, such as the interior, for buyers.

The naval architect for the trailerable 27.8 was designer Fred Bingham (no relation to Joe), who designed some of the Pacific Seacraft's heavy-weather fleet. That was an impressive pedigree: Pacific Seacraft was recognized as one of the best production builders in the world.

"We don't compete against the big boat-building corporations," Joe explained. "Our boating clientele is different. We deal with a person that wants a particular kind of boat.

"A lot of what has kept our business here is that we are very flexible. For another thing, we have to enjoy less profit. We know that from the start. Everything we buy, such as an engine, is one by one, whereas Hunter may buy a truck full. Our savings result from labor, not materials because you don't have the right boat if you skimp on materials."

Joe has sailed his boats extensively, and they reflect his experiences on nearby Lake Superior, a good testing ground for a craft. He settled on the Fred Bingham design because of its seaworthiness (it has offshore capabilities, Bingham advertises) and its nearly full keel design.

"It's a three-quarters full keel," Joe explained, "with a cutaway up front."

He chose this design over a fin keel because he felt that for cruising, "a full keel is a lot more sea-kindly than a fin keel, has a better motion, and tracks better."

"And for trailering, it's much easier to put on and off to launch and haul since the full keel sits on the trailer ramp."

Boat speed? Joe says his full-keel boat is surprisingly fast despite a greater wetted surface. Putting a Bingham 27.8 against other boats convinced him, "You're talking a difference of perhaps a 10th of a knot."

"If I had a choice in a Superior storm, I would go full keel myself. It is more sea kindly and much stronger. Think about it: a fin keel is held on by just a few bolts—and how long can you rack that back and forth?

"The full keel is part of the boat. At least the keel is going to come back home with you."

I thought that over as he continued: "I think that the fin keel was pushed on the public, not by choice, but by production demands because it's a lot easier to manufacture. Think of it: you could basically build a flat boat, jack it up, and then stick on the keel. I worked with Hunter for a few years and looked at standard fin-keel production techniques. With the scoop transom, you could walk right in; it is very easy to fit out. It is designed as a production boat."

Boat building at Bingham Boat Works is mostly one at a time and limited to demand. "If we could build just one boat and do nothing else, it would take three months. Most of the building time is focused on the boat's inside. We can make the hull and deck in six weeks. The finishing off is the time-consuming part."

Nearly everything is done at Bingham's Works. "We made our mold, and we do our own laying up of the hull," Joe told me. The hull thickness of the 27.8 cruiser is surprising. At the sheer, it is 3/8-inches thick. At the waterline, it grows to 5/8 inches. Where the hull flares into the keel, it measures 3/4-inches thick. The thickness is one inch at the bottom—practically a bullet-proof hull.

Bingham fits a 2,665-pound custom-cast lead keel into the keel cavity, set in epoxy putty, so there's no place for water to get in. Over the lead keel, Bingham places layers of fiberglass. "That's with the idea that if you turn turtle, you might want all that lead to stay where it belongs."

The 27.8 is fitted with a Westerbeke 18-horsepower diesel, which will give the boat a respectable top speed under power of 7½ to 8 knots. But a customer can also substitute a Yanmar 18-horsepower diesel since the engine mounts will fit either.

The cutter rig spreads 412 square feet of sail, a lot for a 28-foot cruising craft. But Joe points out that you have three sails to meet a variety of sailing conditions. With two headsails to work with, a sailor can easily set or douse the outer jib on a roller furler. The working jib is club-footed, with reef points.

"We've had people ask why the cutter rig, and I guess it's because we prefer it. We've sailed a cutter, and you can easily reef down when Superior kicks up its heels. There are two reef points in the main. You can put up something in nearly any weather with reef points in the working jib to balance off the boat."

The boat comes with a tiller, but wheel steering is available. Bingham prefers the tiller. "It's simple and strong. Very quick-acting. Wheel steering is fine if you drive a car, but a tiller is a boat to me."

Joe told me he usually sells one or two boats yearly, primarily to sailors in the Superior and Great Lakes area, though one boat is now plying the waters of the Caribbean. "A physician in Michigan bought one of our 27.8 boats, sailed it for a year on Lake Michigan, then put it on a trailer and trucked it down to Florida. His goal was to spend a couple of years in the Caribbean." Joe smiled: "He's been down there ever since."

We walked in the bright July sunshine, talking about boats and sharing experiences. I told Joe about our stormy midnight arrival at the Keweenaw entryway in our 35-foot catamaran. We were sailing almost blind in the fog, and as we neared, we discovered one of the pier lights was out.

We had a close call: we could have ended up on the rocks.

He told me about a boat that wasn't as lucky.

"I fixed a 28-foot cat after it hit the breakwater coming in during adverse conditions. The skipper told me that the pierhead lights were confusing. He turned in the breakwater, but one of his hulls hit. The collision collapsed the bow on the port hull, smashing the stem back about eight inches. Fortunately, he had a watertight compartment upfront. He limped in here, and we fixed it."

"I can't remember his name," Joe said apologetically. "A lot of customers kid me. I can't remember their names, but I always remember the names of boats."

He permitted himself a small smile. "I don't fix customers; I fix boats." ⚙

22

Come Aboard!

---

*It's a dark and stormy day. How about
a nice sail?*

TODAY'S BLUSTERY WIND is at 20 knots, gusting to 25, out of the southwest. On the lake, there are whitecaps, and on the docks, sailors teeter in their boat shoes as they peer out over the choppy waters, wondering if they should go out.

It's gusty, they say, but you know, that's when we like it best.

We'll go.

I see you looking worried. Don't be. This is not Lake Superior, where we have met the dreaded "Three Sisters" waves and survived a derecho with 134 mph. downbursts. Superior can be like that. But this isn't Superior.

A little while ago, I saw a bumper sticker: *"Sail a real lake."* No name was given. But you know which body of water they were talking about. And why we're attracted and maybe even addicted.

Incidentally, I talk about my boat and myself as "we." You see, we communicate with one another and look after each other. We've been through a lot together. It's hard to explain, but boats do talk in their way. They communicate things. A real sailor will understand.

I want you to shove us off when I give the signal. I'll warm up the engine first (always a good idea). I see you're surprised that *Persistence* moves so easily. That's because she's an ultra-lightweight (UL) boat. Also, I try to keep her bottom clean, so she glides easily on her bottom paint.

As we begin moving, I give the engine a little gas and cock the tiller and the engine at the same time. One hand for the rudder and one for the tiller. The prop is now easing us in reverse as we clear the slip. We adjust our course simultaneously with both the tiller and the engine. Hey, look at the control.

Persistence only draws a few inches under her bottom and is skittery in high crosswinds, so for control you need to keep water flowing over her centerboard and rudder. That's so the wind doesn't catch her bow and blow her into the next dock. Or the nearby boat.

Okay, we're in the fairway. The engine pulls us toward the wind, aided by the cocked rudder. We have bags of control in a gusty crosswind situation that is a problem for many skippers. Now, I'll straighten *Persistence,* so she parallels the fairway.

I snick the five-horsepower, two-cycle Nissan into forward gear, give it a little gas and cock both the tiller and the outboard to steer us out parallel with the fairway. See how slick this works?

This crosswind procedure sounds a lot more complicated to explain than in practice. Once you learn how to place your hands and steer both, you will have great control.

When I was on Superior, I found myself berthed in a slip next to a 28-foot keelboat that dwarfed my little sloop. The owner, a university professor from Iowa, was concerned about the heavy crosswind, and he told me that his keelboat did not back up with control. Speeding up his diesel for more power only pushed the transom off to one side. To overcome the problem, he attached dock lines to his sturdy vessel and gave them to his dockside crew to hold. They would help guide the boat into the fairway, where she could back into the wind and then power out onto Superior.

I decided to go first. I warmed up my five-horsepower outboard, snicked it into reverse, reached over to my outboard's steering arm with my right hand, and placed my left hand on the tiller.

The keelboat crew frowned in concern. I had no lines to the dock. No control, or so it seemed.

The crosswind hit as we got out of the lee of the big sailboat. I corrected with both the engine and the tiller, and we glided effortlessly into the fairway. I turned my boat's stern to the wind, then snicked the engine into forward gear. I gave it a victorious shot of gas. The keelboat crew watched in awe. There were no lines, no drama, and it looked so simple that I was a little embarrassed.

Okay, we're moving. Once we straighten out, I will steer straight ahead and give her a burst of power, maybe a third throttle. Notice our control and how easily we accelerate?

A gust hits us, and we bob a bit. We're an ultralight, and you need to get used to movement under you. Nothing serious, and you may come to enjoy *Persistence's* lively feel. We're alive in the wind.

Take the helm and head her directly into the wind. Which way? You'll see it on the telltales, but mostly I want you to feel it on your ears. These excellent direction finders will tell you the wind's location and speed better than anything else. As a small-craft sailor, you must be alert to wind shifts and gusts. Your ears will tell you.

You're doing great! Just keep her headed up. Before we left, I unloosed the shock cords holding the mainsail to the boom and tucked in a reef. Using shock cords to hold down sails is something I learned from Gerry Spiess. I was amazed on *Yankee Girl* that he tucked his jibs down on the bow with the elastic cords. That's where waves pound the boat in a storm. He said it works, and considering the North Atlantic storms he's been in, he was in a position to know. He also uses elastic cords on the boom to hold down the mainsail, which I am now doing. That works great, but I heard a "ping" noise in one storm on Superior, and the flaked main began climbing the mast. I saw the problem: the cords were good, but a stainless steel fitting that held the cords to the boom had popped its rivets. I had to leave the sail flopping around until I got into a nearby harbor.

I will hoist the mainsail from my cockpit seat since my sail controls are leading aft. I don't have to leave the cockpit to go up to the mast. See how easily the main rises? My main runs in a mast slide on nylon and stainless steel sail slugs. I built the sails myself from a design at Sailright.

Please watch your steering as we raise the main. I have battens in the top, and if the wind is not from directly ahead, the sail will catch on the lazy jacks. No big problem; I know how to handle it, but be aware.

OK, I'm coiling the sheet around the winch atop the cabin. All I have to do is pull— and up the mainsail rises to the mast top. I cleat off the sheet beside the winch. See how the boom is set on a gooseneck inside the sail track and moves up and down a bit, too? I'll tighten that and the boom vang, which will tension the sail. Since we're in heavy air, I also tighten up the sail's outhaul. A key to powered-up sailing is to set the main properly, like a wing foil. In today's heavy weather, we want a relatively flat main.

You're doing great, so steer us on a course to port about 45 degrees. Fine. See how the mainsail fills in? We'll have a lively day out here, and you'll enjoy it. You do have your PFD secure, don't you?

Awright, we just caught a gust, and we leaned a little, and that was to be expected. You don't have to grip the tiller so hard.

It's time to raise the jib. I don't have to go forward to the foredeck. I have my sail controls led aft, so all I have to do is let go of the furler tensioning line and pull out the portside jib sheet. See? The 105-percent genoa unrolls like an oversize window shade.

There. You can feel another power surge right away as the headsail digs in.

It's time to turn off our iron genny, and I pull the engine kill switch. When the engine stops, I depress the motor mount lever and press down on the Nissan's top, and the little outboard swings upward on her oversized engine mount. The prop is now out of the water. No drag.

Persistence is powered by an old-fashioned two-cycle engine, one of the best motors ever built for a little sailboat. Many disagree, of course. Four cycles are quiet and refined. But consider the power this little thing puts out for its size: five horsepower. It only weighs 43 pounds.

And it is reliable. I've known a sailor, Gerry Spiess, who used a two-cycle on his *Yankee Girl* to cross the North Atlantic and the South Pacific. He told me waves hit his outboard so hard he worried the engine was torn off. But when the storm cleared, the engine was still on the transom. And it started. If you don't run a two-cycle full out, you get pretty good mileage–we burn about a third of a gallon an hour. One objection to the two cycles is the smoke from the exhaust. That is a problem, and I understand environmentalists' concerns. I thin out my oil-to-gas ratio (yes, you have to premix these), and I use synthetic oil that calls for a higher ratio of gas to oil than average. I also use synthetic oil in my crankcase to reduce friction and gain more power.

A little story: I got caught in a terrible storm on Superior and, in high winds, my boat canted over so far that the engine's prop came out of the water. It went like this: the boat leans, the prop comes up, the engine starts over-revving and screaming, then the boat goes back in the water, the prop slams into the water, the boat shudders, and the engine stops overrevving. Repeat this over and over again—scary stuff. I was worried something might break. When I got back home, I took the engine in for a check-up. I casually mentioned to the mechanic that I was considering getting a four-cycle. "If you had a four-cycle out there, you wouldn't be here now," he said.

We're a windship now, using the power of the wind to get around. Isn't this great? There is no engine noise, just the sound of the waves, the wind, and the water by our hull. We're moving freely. It's like a dance.

I'll take the helm, thanks. See how the tiller falls into my grip? I de-signed it that way, with the right height, length, and even the proper egg-shaped grip that fits my hand.

To build the tiller, I sat in the cockpit and tried various lengths of wood until I figured out the height and size I wanted. Then I shaped the wood to be the right height and distance. For the shape of the grip, I visited hard-ware stores and tried out various types of screwdrivers. The grip on the rounded ones was the worst; the best was the egg-shaped grip since it fits naturally in the hand.

You probably noticed *Persistence's* easy helm. You didn't have to fight the tiller even in gusts, did you? That's because I semi-balanced the rudder blade. Moving water applies light pressure to the front of the blade so that the aft section of the rudder blade does not overpower the helm, which remains light. That sounds much more complicated than it is, like a lot of sailing knowledge.

In the winds today, it's a good idea to use body weight to help power up the boat. *Persistence* sails best flat, not tipping. Today, we'll both sit on the high side. Notice how that helps? Are conditions still too tippy? You will get used to a sailboat's dance with the wind and water. It just takes a little time. If we're still tipping too much for you, my advice is to push down. Hard. *Heh. Heh.*

You will quickly adjust to how a sailboat works with the wind and the waves. It leans from side to side. Leaning is suitable for high winds: it spills air in the sails, the boat comes back up, and you are on your merry way. There are other ways to cope with leaning. One well-known skipper who liked to sail hard with rail-in-the-water lean installed a clinometer to measure the boat's degree of lean. On this device was an ink marking: *At this point, the skipper's wife gets out and walks home.*

Okay, let's get powered up. *Persistence* loves to dance, but there are a few tricks to sailing her. I will adjust the mid-cockpit traveler to set the mainsail without the upper bending off to windward. Think of it as an airplane wing—you don't see many bent wings, do you?

I installed the mainsheet traveler in the cockpit directly in front of me within easy reach to play the gusts. You must step over it to get forward, but this is a sailboat, not a living room. We can easily adjust our main with the traveler's windward sheeting, even in gusts. You'll see.

Here comes one: see the dark area on the water heading toward us? That gust of wind will mean more pressure on the sails. To stay in control, you can partially reef your main and use your jib furler to reduce your foresail. Usually, reefing your sails only takes a minute or two.

It's better to be safe than sorry, so we'll take a sail reduction and sail through the gusts. I adjust the traveler to set a new angle for the sail. I watch the telltales I have sewn on the sails to see that I am achieving the right lift: I know I'm in the groove and powered up if the small pieces of yarn stream back steadily.

Let's take her upwind. I'll crank up the backstay adjuster to tension the jib stay a bit more. Here we go on this little flyer's best point of sail. You probably noticed that as the jib powered up, the bow went down a bit, and the stern came up. The boat feels lively. We're balanced and not dragging the transom in the water that would create a suction to hold us back. A lot of small craft have a problem with a draggy stern.

We're going to do some leaning, but don't be concerned. Look at me: when I worry, you worry. But don't worry until I do. OK?

Enjoy the ride. I'll play the mainsheet to ease off in some of the puffs so we don't lean too much. *Persistence* sails best relatively flat. That's not always possible, but on the other hand, she doesn't like her rail in the water, either. That's for greenhorns. It's showy, and it only slows you down. Besides, you might have someone on board who wants to get off and walk home.

We're having a great time, but it wasn't always this way on this boat. I've been on boats that seemed to know what to do right off and made you feel comfortable. Not here. When I first got *Persistence* in the water, I had a heck of a time learning her ways: she'd go sideways when I wanted to go forward, didn't seem to want to point, and at times seemed, well, slow. But over the years, I've modified her, and she has always responded for the better. The boat I originally built is not the boat you have under you today.

Like a family or friends, wooden sailboats don't get older—they only get better. It takes some understanding and love. And work.

Now we're heading back. Doesn't time fly when you're having fun on the water? I'll bet you didn't think once about the office! ☸

23

Amazing Gulls

They soar and jink unloved across endless skies

"I storm the golden gates of day.
I wing the silver lanes of night.
I plumb the deep for finny prey,
On wave I sleep in tempest height.
Conceived was I by sea and sky,
Their elements are fused in me.
Of brigand birds that float and fly
I am the freest of the free."

—From *"The Grey Gull"* by Robert Service

TOWERING HIGH ABOVE the Sawtooth Mountains, the dark storm clouds rolled in swiftly—too swiftly. I glanced northward. It would be a close race for my 20-foot centerboard sloop and me.

Any old port in a storm. As I dashed past the entryway, I saw that the tiny harbor was guarded only by a low-lying sandbar—scant protection.

I clambered forward on the deck and dropped Danforth anchors in a classic V-shaped pattern.

Whoom! Downbursts hit my boat, canting it from side to side, fighting the anchors.

Turning around, I realized I was not alone. Near the water's edge stood a band of gulls, bobbing up and down in the blasts—watching me.

Vroom. I braced myself as the gale began to show its teeth.

We canted sideways, vibrating, and rattling in the wind, then righted ourselves.

I snuck a peek at my feathery friends—did they get blasted off? I saw they had lined up in a row to face the wind, ducking their heads down and putting their tails up.

I realized that the gulls used their bodies as airfoils to make the wind press their tiny feet into the sand. Some wobbled drunkenly in the gusts, but quickly regained their balance, maybe only a feather or two out of place.

They remained at their posts, like good soldiers, until the storm abated. Then they fluttered away without a backward glance.

They're wind machines worthy of any sailor's study with distinctive V-shaped, high-aspect-ratio wings. Gulls can shape and reshape their wing angles and even individual feathers for the best aerodynamics.

They hover, soar the thermals, and suddenly fold their wings, dive into the water, and become aquatic. When they bob up again, they are airborne with just a few flaps of their wings.

Whoever designed these birds was a genius.

Gulls soar endlessly on their high-aspect wings.

Photo/Marlin Bree

But gulls are not entirely appreciated by all. "Wharf rats," say some waterfront critics. "Nuisances."

Boat owners are hard hit, and I sympathize, gull darn it. Pardon. The seabirds have left more than their calling cards on *Persistence's* bright-finished teak deck and varnished mahogany cabin top.

I take care of any birdy problem as I do my pre-sail inspection. When I arrive at my boat, I get a pail of lake water, splash the boat down, wipe the poo off with paper towels, and seal the used wipes into a disposable plastic bag.

Some boaters have tried other methods of dealing with gulls, including scaring them off with old CDs or cloth streamers fluttering from spreaders. There are fake owls and lengths of ropes, but gulls are smart and quickly adapt.

Revenge is not far behind. One does not mock the birds.

But even the gulls' leavings pale by comparison to ducks. Have you ever seen a racing-style sailboat with its aft cockpit open nearly to the water? Without a transom, ducks can walk right in and make themselves at home. And more.

To me, the solution is to coexist with nature. Frankly, the gulls were here first—long before boaters. You share the air and water with them. What the gulls put down, the lowly skipper wipes up.

They almost disappeared. In the late 19th century, gulls' pretty feathers, plumage, and even entire wings adorned women's millinery to such an extent that gulls were in danger of becoming extinct. But thanks to protective wildlife legislation, gulls have made a big-time comeback.

Gulls are medium to large birds, and the largest gull (the Great Black-backed Gull) spreads a wingspan of almost six feet. There are 45 gull species globally; the most common is the Herring Gull (wingspan up to 57 inches). Frankly, it takes a real expert to tell gulls apart.

They fly exceedingly well, are good gliders and hoverers on thermals, and can achieve speeds up to about 45 mph. A gull has thousands of feathers, weighing more than its ultra-light hollow bones, and spends 10 percent of its waking hours preening them. That's not for beauty but to keep flyable.

Gulls have remarkable instincts and intelligence. Watch a flight of gulls and see how they jink about the skies silently and in unison, no gull bumping into another, and they achieve this with no apparent signals. They do "talk" when there's danger—or food. People don't understand them, however.

Gulls are good parents and will teach a young gull how to prepare difficult-to-eat seafood, such as clams. Parents fly high with the clams and drop them on a hard surface, breaking the clam open. And there is dinner.

Gulls also hold their own "gull dances." They bob up and down on the ground, sometimes in a dance line, with their little feet pounding the earth. The gulls are simulating the sound of the patter of rain on the ground, making the worms come out. A fine gull meal.

And there's Sam, the Scottish gull renowned for his trick of walking into a seafront store, looking to see if anyone is watching, then going to the same rack and picking out the same brand of chips, day after day. Carrying his prize to a nearby parking lot, Sam tears open the bag to share his loot with fellow gulls, always the same brand of cheese-flavored chips.

Gulls still have a mystery about them. Scientists have yet to figure out how gulls know where to migrate each fall when they fly thousands of miles south, sometimes as far as Mexico or South America. Scientists think gulls' expert navigation involves sensing electromagnetic forces and observations of the sun and the stars—with a built-in GPS.

Migrations are tough on the birds. Only about one in four gulls makes it back.

Gulls have long had a place in folklore and legends. Ocean sailors have seen the gull as a harbinger of good news, probably because sighting a gull at sea on a long voyage means the land is close. Old sailors believed that no one should harm a gull. Some believe that the souls of their departed shipmates were reincarnated as gulls.

One gull legend is about Lake Superior sailor Al Wray of Thunder Bay, a World War II battle survivor who sailed to Thompson Island every chance he got with his wife, Georgiana. As Al grew older, he told his friends, "When I kick the bucket, I'm coming back as a seagull."

When Al died, a large white gull appeared in Georgiana's window and would not go away. As a funeral procession of boats carried Al's ashes out to his beloved island, mourners heard the fluttering of large wings. A blindingly white seagull flew overhead, wheeling near friends' boats, cavorting in the skies to the island.

"I suspect Al is spending his time in paradise," a fellow boater explained. ✸

24

Huzzah! Les Voyageurs

*They paddled across a wilderness—
and into legend*

No water, no weather, ever stopping
The paddle or the song.
—Voyageur's saying

IN THE SHADOW of Mount Josephine, the old fur fort's gleaming stockade nestled along the harbor's edge. As I looked from my boat across the bay, I tried to imagine what a welcome sight Grand Portage must have been as the voyageurs ended their 1,200-mile watery route from New France. They had paddled and portaged their fragile canoes halfway across a wilderness continent.

Crossing Lake Superior, they braved storms, high waves, and unpredictable weather in birchbark canoes. These were not the typical Indian-style craft but 40-foot canoes large enough to hold a dozen men and tons of cargo, yet light enough to carry across the 36 portages between Montreal and Grand Portage.

The heavily loaded canoe brigades set out early each May to carry goods into the wilderness. Their westward route lay along the great arc of the lake on the rugged Canadian north shore—the one *Persistence* and I would be sailing as soon as the weather let up.

For their deeds, the voyageurs were idolized throughout the world.

Legends grew not only about their stamina and strength but for their brav-
ery in the face of hardship and danger. Stories were told and retold around
campfires about how they reveled in harsh adventures, ignored pain and
suffering, and laughed in the face of danger.

I could picture them —men big-shouldered and heavily muscled from
paddling their canoes. They'd be laughing and talking, their distinctive
long caps twitching from side to side—a jolly bunch, outlandish in their
jokes and tales.

"You look like a voyageur," someone once told me. *Hmm.* At 5 feet 7
inches, I am not the tallest of people.

"Except," my friend added, "you should be twice as wide in the shoulders."

He did not add that if I were a typical voyageur, at my age I'd be
suffering from a hernia or two, chronic back pain, joint aches, and pains,
or—most likely—dead.

As I walked through the fur fort's gate, I looked at the distinctive
wooden stockade walls. These were high and had sharpened points at
the top. The stockade and the log buildings inside the heavy walls are all
replicas. The original fort long ago fell into dust.

The fur trading post began in 1768, about the time of the American
Revolution, and became the inland headquarters of the Montreal fur-trading organization, the North West Company.

I met the National Park Service's David Cooper at Grand Portage
National Monument. "Native people were using Grand Portage hundreds
to thousands of years before the arrival of the Europeans," Cooper told me.
He was talking about the "grand portage," known as the old Great Carrying Place, a largely uphill, rugged nine-mile trail to the waterways leading
deep into Canada. "The Indians used it for trading purposes and seasonal
movement. There was a lot of travel up and down Superior."

That surprised me. I did not think of Superior as a well-used water
highway before the voyageurs.

He assured me it was. "It was amazing how far people went
in a canoe as part of their annual rounds. It was not uncomon
to travel from Grand Portage to Sault Ste. Marie by canoe.

The Sault was at one time the cultural center for the Ojibway people."

In the distance across the bay, Grand Portage Island was still wreathed in fog. I could see mist layers descending from Hat Point. We walked out onto a long wooden dock.

"Is this where the voyageurs landed?"

"We don't know for certain. There's a place nearby that makes more sense."

"Show me?"

We made our way along the front of the fort and crossed a small river. I looked down at a beach. It was sandy, unlike the bay's rocky areas.

"They would run their canoes into the shallows. The voyageurs would leap out to keep the canoes from grounding and damaging their bottoms. Then they'd unload."

He nodded his head in a northeasterly direction. Across the bay, bobbing at the marina, lay my boat. I could barely make out its mast. The wooded hills rose behind; beyond was the Witch Tree, a spiritual place.

"Out there was the last landfall before Grand Portage. Beyond Hat Point, they'd clean themselves up, get ready for the final leg, and come around singing and racing to the beach. If they were the first brigade in, the shores would be lined with people waiting for the news from Montreal and firing guns. It would have been a great scene."

Not only did the voyageurs arrive here, but so did the Northmen in their canoes. The rendezvous would begin a big party—the only one of the year for some Northmen.

"But officials had to keep them away from the Montreal men because they fought like cats and dogs."

I could imagine this grassy knoll filled with the brawling, rowdy canoe men.

Cooper explained: "The Montreal men were the lower end of the fur trade society. They were the greenhorns and were referred to derisively as pork eaters by the Northmen, as they had lard as a part of their rations. They were considered tenderfeet, even though the 1,200-mile paddle and brutal portages were no easy trip. Anyone who could do that would be no greenhorn by today's standards."

I thanked Cooper and explored the fort on my own. Walking around the southwest corner of the stockade, I saw a shelter cloth attached to one side of the stockade, a small tent, and a fire site.

It was a Northman's encampment. With a paddle in his hand, nearby was Northman Karl Koster.

"Is that, er, a dress you're wearing?"

He was only momentarily taken aback. "Long shirt," the senior interpreter corrected me.

He explained that the long shirt, breechclout, and knee-high leggings are preferable to traditional men's trousers. "You go through the woods a lot better."

Karl had paddled in canoes and portaged through the woods in his work as a winterer in the northwest.

"The voyageurs paddled 40 to 60 strokes a minute," he said, handing me his paddle. "And they paddled 12 to 18 hours a day."

I hefted the paddle, surprised that it was so lightweight. It was hand-carved out of lightweight cedar—a wood that my boat was made of—and was small, allowing for a fast pace.

Karl explained: "A wider paddle, and you're going to get more resistance and give you a little more upper body wear."

The Montreal birch-bark canoe could be 40 feet long and carry 4 to 5 tons. The voyageurs ended up floating only six inches above the water. "You don't need a long paddle," Karl observed.

"Even when you get ten strong guys in a loaded canoe, you can hardly move from a standing stop. The whole thing is momentum."

He demonstrated the slow beginning strokes—little chops—then gradually increased the length and power.

"When she gets kicking, you don't stop. You keep the momentum going."

They paddled long, hard hours in fragile birch-bark canoes, trying not to let Superior's storms stop them.

"Most were just farm boys out for the adventure and the scenery. It wasn't the pay that kept them coming back."

"Mon ami," he said, holding up his paddle. "Everyone knows of the voyageur's love of paddles. You even sleep with it."

On a fog-shrouded day, the author examines a replica birchbark voyageur canoe at Grand Portage National Monument.

Photo/Marlin Bre

The canoe house was a handsome two-story wooden building with a large door facing the bay. Here, the canoes could be built or, equally important, rebuilt.

Inside were birch-bark canoes, large and small, including voyageurs' canoes. I also found a pack of the type that a voyageur would carry. I tried to heft just one.

I grunted. I could hardly lift it a short distance from the ground.

The pack contained 60 to 65 beaver pelts and weighed 90 pounds. Voyagers carried these on portages uphill and down along rough woodland trails from lake to lake.

"They weren't considered much of a man if they could not carry two of them on their backs," interpreter Joyce Blanton told me.

"There were three things a voyageur had to be: they could be 5 foot 6 inches to 5 foot 8 inches tall; it was a requirement that they not be able to swim. Another requirement was that they had to know how to sing."

She explained that they had to sing to keep time and could not be tall, or their legs would take up too much room in the canoe. They'd also weigh too much.

And certifying that they could not swim?

That way, the company was confident that if a canoe tipped over, the voyageurs wouldn't swim to shore—and refuse to come back.

But in the old days, many boys grew up wanting to be voyageurs.

"It's what they lived for, was to be a voyageur," she said.

25

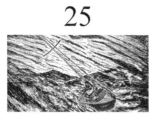

Secrets of Survival

How did a 20-foot sailboat stand up to 134 mph winds?

THE DAY HAD BEGUN FOGGILY. *Persistence* was tied behind a rusty barge in Grand Portage, Minnesota harbor, not far from the Canadian-US border, and the damned engine would not start, which surprised me. My one-cylinder two-stroke Nissan always fired up, sooner or later.

Last night, I had been treated to the worst electrical storm I'd ever been in. Lightning crackled about me, and rain sheets hammered down my cabin roof. This morning, I tried to dry the cockpit with my boat sponge and paper towels, but everything was soaked. The humidity was high, very high. My glasses kept steaming up.

Increasingly hard yanks on the outboard's starting cord did nothing— I only got a few muted whuffs and huffs. Beads of water stood on the cowling. I removed the cowling, changed the spark plug, and checked the gas filter, pressure bulb, and gas tank. All OK. Nothing was out of the ordinary except that I noticed the powerhead was damp. Beneath its protective cowling, the engine itself had a moisture problem.

Panting from the exertion, I went below into the cabin and made myself a latte with my espresso maker. All good little boats should have espresso makers.

Then, back at getting the outboard going. After an hour and strong pulls, the outboard finally started with a smidgeon of blue smoke and a raspy noise. It happily settled down to a steady idle.

My confidence was getting restored. We were late on our schedule, but we were moving.

Out on Lake Superior, the heavy pea-soup fog started to burn off, and NOAA weather on my VHF radio broadcast that today would be the warmest of the year, July 4, 1999. I was anxious to be on my way across the U.S./ Canada border.

I had my Canpass ready. To check-in, I had to report via my VHF radio to the Canadian Coast Guard. The paperwork was already done. It would be an easy run for me and my 20-foot sailboat.

My destination was a tiny harbor inside an island at the mouth of Thunder Bay. Canadian boating friends told me Thompson Island was a cruising destination not to miss. It lay just across the border.

The sun emerged, and the fog began to burn off to the east, but I noticed dark clouds looming over the Sawtooth Mountain Range. I thought I heard something on my radio—snatches of words, but I could not make them out because of engine noise. Two-cycle outboards are rackety. Minutes later, I overheard another VHF message that a sailboat with three people on board had overturned in very high winds north of me.

What was going on? I turned up the throttle.

I had Thomson Island in view and figured I'd make it in 20 minutes. Easy.

Out of nowhere came a howling noise. The sky grew dark, and the wind hummed in the rigging, higher and higher in pitch until it became an ear-piercing shriek. Winds grabbed *Persistence* by the mast and shoved us around, side to side and back and forth.

To the north lay a tiny island. But I couldn't power into that much wind with a five-horsepower outboard. Spar Island remained out of reach.

I turned my boat's stern to the wind. That way, I had the wind bearing down on the boat's 20-foot length, not her vulnerable and tippy beam.

Running with the wind, *Persistence's* bow came up and rode high like a powerboat. We sped out toward Superior's open waters.

Suddenly, I felt a heavy wind blast, worse than the rest. The whole boat shivered, then I saw the bow depress and stuff itself into a wave. We stopped. The stern flipped up and catapulted me headfirst into the cabin below. I ducked to miss hitting the hatch cover but slammed into the starboard bulkhead. I hit my head.

When I returned to consciousness, I lay sprawled atop equipment boxes. My head and right ankle hurt. I raised my head, adjusted my glasses, and saw my alarm clock on my portside nav station slowly levitate, bounce off the cabin top, and come to rest on my cabin's starboard side.

The smoke-colored plexiglass portlight had turned a beautiful, bright, luminous green. I admired the color only for a moment.

We were lying on our side, mast in the water, and not getting back up.

My outboard screamed—the propeller was out of the water.

I clambered back into the cockpit in time to see heavy rubber fenders vibrate, bounce up and down, and fly into the sky. Superior had furrows of miles-long foam, like huge haymows, writhing back and forth.

I leaned over the side to use my weight to lever the vessel upright. But my wrestling match with the storm wasn't working. The mast top stubbornly stuck a few feet above the water, slowly moving up and down.

Suddenly, the boat bounded upright with a whump noise and a splashing sound. The mast flogged back and forth. I grabbed a lifeline to steady myself as my boat shook off the water. I don't know what had been pinning *Persistence* on her side, but it was gone now.

Upright, the boat lowered the prop into the water. We raced further into Superior—and deeper into the storm.

We could not live out here. When I sensed the blasts had diminished, I timed the waves, twisted the throttle flat out, and shoved the tiller to starboard. The engine snarled; *Persistence* turned to port, and, to my surprise, we fought our way into Sand Island's lee.

The island shouldered off most of the high winds, so it was time to try a balancing act. I remained at the helm, one hand on the throttle, the other on the tiller, and fed the engine just enough gas to keep us into the wind but off the rocks. So long as I could maintain our position, with wind shoving us out to sea and the engine pushing us back to shore, we were safe—for the time being.

I started to shiver. I was dressed in long johns, a fleece sweater, a fleece-lined Helly Hanson boating jacket, wool pants, and wool socks, but dammit, I was cold. I glanced inside the cabin to make out my Stearns survival suit with quarter-inch foam neoprene between heavy nylon shells inside and out. That would warm me nicely. It was only feet away in the port side quarter berth, but I could not reach it. I could not leave the helm.

The waves were kicking up whitecaps. Thompson Island was not far—it was time to make my move.

With my hand on the throttle, I powered past the pinnacles of wave-lashed rock. But running alongside the seaward side of the island, I could not find the harbor entry. There were no marking or channel indicators, just wilderness bluffs, and trees.

I found a channel between the island's tip and another bit of land. Was this the entryway to the harbor?

Revving up the engine, I attempted to force *Persistence* through the fast-moving water, but I was tossed back several times. It was like trying to paddle up a whitewater mountain stream.

Suddenly, we were through. My speeding boat speared an oncoming wave, burying my bow. Chill water raced back along the cabin top and hit me in the face. The drenching woke me up.

Ping! I heard something break, and I saw my flaked mainsail begin to climb the mast. A stainless steel fitting on the boom had failed, and the fingers of the wind were pushing up the big sail. I loosened the mainsheet and let the boom flop back and forth, along with the partially raised sail. I couldn't leave the helm to fix them. They'd have to take it—just like me.

The waves had grown. Atop one set, I could look around: more islands. But not the one I wanted.

I needed to find my safe harbor. Fast.

Atop an onrushing growler, I changed course. We ran with the waves, sometimes atop one, sometimes in the trough, and headed back for that whitewater channel.

Rocky slopes hurried past me. Beyond one crag, I saw something shining. Up high above the trees, they looked like crosses. I squinted to clear my focus; unmistakably, they were sailboats masts—just the tips of them.

On one side was a high outcrop of rock, and on the other, a spruce-covered hill. And in between, still blue water. The channel.

I had found blessed, beautiful Thompson harbor.

Once securely tied up in the harbor, I went below to check the cabin. Everything loose within the boat was scattered everywhere. I began moving gear around, unfastening bags from beside the centerboard trunk.

The bilge had inches of water in which cans of bean soup and Dinty Moore stew floated about. Had the hull sprung a leak?

I bailed the water and dried the bilge with my large boat sponge. I held my breath and waited. Then I checked again: no new trickles of water. I was safe, for now.

What had happened? I remembered all too vividly what had happened in the storm. When the boat was on its beam ends and the mast tipped in and out of the water, I saw spray gush through the open centerboard trunk inside the cabin. Was that where the water came from?

I found my alarm clock and my wristwatch. The clock had flown from one side of the cabin to the other and had stopped running. I checked the batteries and shook the clock. It worked when it stood upright. My wristwatch had been torn from my wrist when I fell, and it was missing a strap pin, which lay somewhere in the bilge. I put the watch in my jacket pocket.

It seemed incredible that I'd survived a storm the likes of which I'd never encountered before—and hoped never to come across again.

But the incident wasn't over. I completed my voyage into the wilderness of Canada's north shore, but when I returned home with my boat trailered behind my Suzuki Sidekick 4 x 4, I was puzzled at what I had encountered. In the islands and along the Canadian north shore where I sailed, boaters and waterfront people who witnessed or were in the storm regarded the event as a large, freak thunderstorm. Impressive and dangerous, to be sure.

But what was it?

News accounts began to fill the picture: the storm had not begun somewhere near where I was sailing but had moved out of Minnesota's western part. Trees snapped, and power lines went down in winds clocked as high as 91 mph. About 80 miles north and west of where I had been boating,

The Boundary Waters Canoe Area Wilderness (BWCAW) had caught the worst of the storm's impact, which devastated about half a million acres and damaged 2.5 million trees. It was "one of the largest North American forest disturbances in recorded history," a *Minneapolis Star Tribune* article reported. "Wild downdrafts" resulted in one of the biggest blowdowns ever recorded, wrote Paul Douglas, meteorologist for the *Star Tribune*.

News media called it the storm of the century.

Since I had served in U.S. Army Intelligence during the "Cold War," I knew experts in aerial photography could determine wind speed from the photographed evidence on the ground. I sent photographs to be analyzed, and I was told: "Winds in excess of 100 mph."

Exploring the Internet, I first learned from the Gunflint Ranger District, Grand Marais, Minnesota, that the storm was a "derecho." Toofarnorth (the moniker of the ranger station) explained that a derecho is a convective windstorm consisting of not one but a complex of thunderstorms—a rare occurrence. The straight-line winds had caused a blowdown of about 477,000 acres in the Superior National Forest. It had taken only 30 minutes.

In Thunder Bay, Ontario, residents were awed by the violent winds—and the green sky. A meteorologist explained that when the sun shines down on the top of the clouds, the light gets "refracted down—just like a prism," with a green color. In Canada, the storm came to be called "The Green Storm."

NOAA was setting up its website, *About Derechos.* There's a segment called Notable Derechos, and the one I'm in is under the category, **Noteworthy Events.** Drop down to the *July 4-5, 1999 Derecho, "The Boundary Waters-Canadian Derecho."* I learned that what hit me was one of the farthest north "progressive derechos" recorded. And one of the worst.

Derechos barnstorm across regions with straight-line winds of *60 to 100 mph.* That's bad enough, but there's more: Out of these high-speed thunderstorms come *downbursts* and *microbursts* of heavy, chilly air. Slamming downward from squall lines, the downbursts hug the ground below, blasting anything in their path.

NOAA reported that downburst speeds are "well in excess and perhaps as much as *double the gust front speed.*"

But Derechos can change—for the worse. NOAA said that Derechos *speed up over water* since nothing obstructs them, such as hills and forests.

Onboard my boat, over the racket of my outboard, I wondered at snatches of a VHF report that a sailboat had overturned in Thunder Bay Harbor with three people in the water. I also later learned that Sally, from Voyager's Marina in Grand Portage, had tried to warn me on the VHF that something "big" was headed my way. She had advised me to find an island to hide behind—a message I had never received.

I remember an intense wind jumping over the Sawtooth Mountains and moving faster than other Superior storms I have sailed through. The gusts played the shrouds like a musical instrument, quickly growing higher in tone and louder, culminating in a loud, unearthly shriek. My boat twisted about as if a giant hand grabbed the mast and swung it around. The wind made the boat speed up so much that the bow lifted like a speedboat. Something landed on the bow, and the front end of my boat submerged. I watched it being pushed under the water. We stopped as if somebody had hit the brakes. The aft section of the boat flipped up in a near pitchpole, tossing me inside the cabin. I flew inside, hitting my head against a bulkhead. *Persistence* was knocked down on her beam ends and would not come back up. The mast tip danced in and out of the water. Then, whatever was pinning us down, let up—and *Persistence* bounced upright.

Later, for *Wake of the Green Storm,* I quoted meteorologist Paul Douglas, who estimated the derecho that hit where I was sailing had winds as high as 134 mph. I quoted him on that figure.

I wondered: Why does Lake Superior brew up such wild storms? Paul told me that because Lake Superior is so deep, it stays cold well into the summer, creating a massive differential in air temperatures between the chilly waters and the relatively warm air passing overhead, increasing the odds of wild thunderstorms and high winds.

He added, "Of all the Great Lakes, I would least want to be caught on Superior."

NOAA's web pages, *About Derechos,* reported in words, photographs, and computer imagery the power and strength of the storm's straight-line winds. NOAA identified the danger of downbursts from the wall cloud that ushered in the storm. NOAA had clocked the overland winds at over 80 miles per hour but reported that the microbursts slamming down from the wall cloud could develop winds *twice the straight-line speed.*

Months after the derecho ravaged the boreal forests of North America, workers cleared some roads, and I could drive my 4 x 4 to the west of where I had been sailing. I was amazed at the devastation—and something else. Straight-line winds had toppled old-growth pines, snapped some in half, and torn others out of the earth by their roots. I anticipated seeing hilltops scalped of trees, but not valleys. I thought that the straight-line winds would skip over the valleys. Instead, I saw giant pines lying in a circle with their tops pointing outward from the center in one valley. It was as if a giant fist had come down from the heavens and smashed this valley flat. And headed out to sea where I was.

The evidence is still there on the earth if anyone doubts derecho's power. ☸

Photo/ Marlin Bree

About the **Persistance**

Traditional wooden boats are individual wood pieces held to-gether with mechanical fasteners, such as bolts, nails, and screws. My boat is a monocoque hull—where everything is fastened to everything else, making it solid, stout, but ultra-light. I did not spare the epoxy when I glued up the hull and added fillets and gussets for extra strength. If you rap the hull with your knuckle, you'll be rewarded with a satisfying "thunk" sound. That's solid construction.

Persistence is 20 feet long and 7 feet 4 inches wide. I laid up the hull with three layers of one-eighth-inch Western Red Cedar veneers in a triple diagonal pattern. The heaviest woods, such as inch-thick white oak, went below for the keel and keel-son. The keel has a unique feature: My friend Gerry Spiess not only donated a few "good luck" pieces of equipment from his Atlantic voyage in *Yankee Girl* but also signed his name in indelible ink to my boat's oaken keel.

I built the laminated stem out of oak. All woods are glued and coated with marine epoxy, and the hull and cabin are wrapped in six-ounce fiberglass cloth coated with epoxy. The bottom is finished off in several additional epoxy-graphite coatings.

I have 46 inches of headroom in the cabin. There are two aisles on either side of the 18-inch-high open centerboard trunk, each 71 inches long and 18 inches wide. To port lies the navigation station; to starboard, the galley area. I lift a floor-board and insert it between the nav station and the CB trunk to work as my writing desk while sitting on my forward v-berth.

In a small boat's cabin, the way to get around is to crawl or duck waddle. You get used to it.

For weight control below, I strapped two heavy-duty (and heavyweight) marine batteries securely atop the keel. Midships, a heavy centerboard case holds the 3/8ths-inch-thick steel centerboard. Aft of the CB and directly atop the keel in a well lie two Danforth anchors, one a lunch-hook and the other, a heavy-duty anchor with chain leader, on 150 feet of stretchy 3/8ths nylon anchor line. Occasionally, I carry an 18-pound "mudder" mushroom anchor.

Persistence has several other ways to enhance her righting ability. I built the cabin sides within six inches of the hull's beam. In a knockdown, the cabin sides would provide extra floatation for support, and the boat would not turn turtle and "flop" into the water, mast pointing to the bottom. That worked during the Green Storm. *Persistence* at times teetered on her cabin sides, the portlights fully emersed. But she didn't go all the way over, despite the storm's best efforts.

Some small craft have rub rails of plastic or hard rubber. I made mine out of inch-thick Sitka Spruce. I crafted rub rails on each side, tapering them at the front and the back to give the hull's straight sheer a little more grace. These wood rub rails would protect the hull from damage from too-hot docking, other boats—and outrageous fortune. The sculpted rail would add floatation if the boat got knocked down—a built-in "life preserver" around the beam. I don't know how much floatation two planks of wood 18 feet long by one-inch thick by 3 inches in height would add to a boat, but all I can say is that it worked.

I took off the mast crane to foam *Persistence's* mast, spraying foam in the uppermost mast section. During the "Green Storm," *Persistence* was severely tested. Knocked down repeatedly on her beam ends, we "bounced" up and down as the mast floatation levered us upright. After being tossed belowdecks along the cabin side, I could feel that upward thrust. At first, I did not fully understand what was happening, but I finally figured it out: The mast was pushing us back up out of the water.

For additional ballast control, I removed the floorboards and tossed cartons of goods, food, water, tools, and supplies into the bilge alongside the CB trunk on the boat bottom. On top of the pile went lightweight sleeping bags, blankets, and clothing bags. To keep this weight—now ballast—in place, I stretched bungee cords from the top of the centerboard case to the cabin sole. The result is that the weight is as low as possible and removed from the boat's ends. When the bow submerged in big waves, the boat bounced back more quickly without extra weight in the bow holding it back. It only takes a few minutes to lighten the bow and the stern.

I worried about the outboard. The outboard's prop was repeatedly yanked out of the water when the boat went over on its side. The engine racketed madly—overrevving without cooling water pumped into the powerhead. I worried the engine might overheat and blow up. But somehow, it kept taking a beating and kept on ticking.

I still have that 43-pound outboard, and as I enter my workshop, I stop to pat the little two-cycle affectionately. The engine did not fail me, and I will never forget its faithful duty. Small craft sailors are like that.

And if anyone asks about the survivability of the small craft, adequately built and manned, I could tell them: You don't need a big boat. It's not what you have—it's what you do with what you have that can make all the difference.

26

Lure of the High Ice

Cloud Nine *conquers the Northwest Passage*

THERE'S A RULE OF THUMB that veteran ice skippers like Roger Swanson come to understand about the Arctic: You don't know what to expect until you get there, and—here's the tricky part—if you wait until you know what to expect, you might be too late to get what you expect.

In 2005, Swanson's 57-foot Bowman ketch, *Cloud Nine,* was trapped in Arctic sea ice during his second attempt to transit the Northwest Passage. He escaped with the help of a Canadian icebreaker. He later learned that the threatening ice pack would have blown out if he'd waited two more days. "But September 13 was too late in the season to wait. I decided I'd had enough," he said.

The dream stayed with him to cross the top of the world through the infamous route in his sailboat.

Swanson was tantalized by emails from an Arctic friend that the Northwest Passage might be open, though another report said that the central part was only "slightly better than normal."

On June 28, 2007, *Cloud Nine* headed north from the Virgin Islands.

The Northwest Passage is a long-sought sea route through water-ways in the Canadian Arctic Archipelago between the Atlantic and Pacific Oceans. The Passage has been tantalizingly open at times to lure sailors, but the water routes were, and are, unpredictable with shifting ice and winds that build up ice packs that can crush vessels.

Explorers had searched for a maritime route for centuries, with a southern passage finally discovered in 1854. Norwegian Roald Amundsen made the first complete transit from 1903 through 1906. Part of his technique was to sail as far as he could until his heavily reinforced wooden boat was frozen in and remain in place until the area thawed the following year, then sail again.

Not so fortunate was the ill-fated 1845 expedition of Sir John Franklin in his lavishly equipped two-ship expedition. A century-and-a-half later, the boats were found—under the ice. The grim story emerged that the ships were ice-bound in 1846 near King William Island and unable to break loose. All aboard perished. There were reports of cannibalism.

After a stopover in Halifax, Nova Scotia, *Cloud Nine* left on July 19 with Swanson's wife, Gaynelle Templin, and four other crew members. In the Straight of Belle Isle, they encountered their first ice; gale force winds hurried them around Cape Bauld. Fog plagued them, and caution was necessary because although large icebergs usually show up on radar, the smaller ones and the bergy bits don't.

On this third attempt, *Cloud Nine* crossed the Arctic Circle on August 2 while headed north in the Davis Strait, off the west coast of Greenland. On one occasion, Swanson recalled, "we counted seventy-nine bergs all visible at the same time. Motoring through these magnificent castles of ice is a humbling, but incredibly exhilarating, experience."

Working their way around the northern edge of the ice pack at Baffin Bay, they reached 74 degrees 53 minutes north latitude, the northernmost point of their trip. Their radar failed, and their magnetic compass wasn't dependable because the magnetic North Pole was so close.

"Steering was difficult with fog, no compass, no radar, and only our GPS," Swanson said.

Cloud Nine passes an Arctic iceberg.

Photo/David Thoreson

Roger told me that *Cloud Nine* was an ordinary cruising sailboat with no extra reinforcement for protection against the ice. For power, it had a single diesel engine.

When *Cloud Nine* was constructed in England, boatbuilders did not know the strength of fiberglass, so they added extra layers. Gaynelle thought the sailboat had fiberglass thicker than most boats. The hull was old-fashioned solid fiberglass from the keel up to the gunwales—no foam core.

"The ice just bounced off," she said.

The hull was quiet, too. "We did not hear that much noise from ice scraping along the hull in the ice fields," she said. "It was more like the sound of skaters on an ice rink."

They often could not sail with the towering bergs around them but ran under their diesel engine, a small four-cylinder that chugged faithfully along. "It sounded like it would drone on forever," she said. In the ice, they usually powered at a conservative four knots.

Ice presented a unique problem. When *Cloud Nine* was running through fog banks, Gaynelle checked the below-decks radar screen. It showed all clear. Nothing ahead.

But when she arrived in the cockpit to take over the helm, she saw a giant iceberg loom out of the patchy fog. She could not determine its height because of a fog layer around its bottom and another layer around its top. "That got my attention," she said.

Immediately, they changed course. Gaynelle rechecked the radar: Again, the huge berg did not appear on the screen. "We knew icebergs showed up sometimes—and sometimes not."

Roger Swanson at the helm of *Cloud Nine*

Photo/ David Thoreson

In Cambridge Bay, on the southeast corner of Victoria Island, the crew picked up a new radar and set off in the fog, hurrying because northerly winds still could bring down the ice pack. Dodging heavy storms, they sailed through the Beaufort Sea, the Chukchi Sea, the Bering Strait, and the Bering Sea to get to Dutch Harbor at Unalaska, Alaska.

They took 73 days to complete the 6,600-mile passage, including 3,433 nautical miles between their northward crossing and their southward recrossing of the Arctic Circle.

Cloud Nine became the first US sailboat to transit the Northwest Passage from east to west. It was also the first American sailing vessel to complete the passage in one year.

At age 76, Swanson, who lived in Dunnell, Minnesota, and described himself as a "hog farmer," became the oldest skipper to make the problematic Passage across the top of the world that had eluded navigators for centuries. He did it with an "ordinary sailboat" and a down-home crew with no professional sailors. ✿

Epilogue | The Welcome Island

A place in the mind and the heart

AS EVENING DESCENDED, the wind died, and the cove's water was smooth as glass, mirroring the pines and the rocky ledges. The trees turned golden and cast blue shadows in the sun's lowering rays.

I was on Thompson Island. I had found it, more or less, by accident.

Hours before, I had been searching for this tiny island on Superior's open waters. Instead, I was surprised by a sudden storm. The winds howled, the waves grew, and my 20-foot centerboard sloop was in the grip of a rare, progressive derecho.

Now, around me lay calm, blue water surrounded by steep slopes. The wind was gone—and I knew why.

High hills and densely wooded terrain isolated me. The storm was still raging on the open waters, but the island shouldered off the storm's blast.

Here it was summer again. Bright. And warm.

When I arrived in the harbor, my mainsail was halfway up the mast, the boom was bounding from side to side, and I was soaked, miserable, and shivery. I saw boats tied up along the bulwarks that served as a dock. As I got closer, I saw that there was no space left.

"Raft up here," a friendly Canadian boater hollered, waving his hands. I could tie up alongside another boat.

"Got a line?"

I tossed him one. Another problem came up.

"I lost all my fenders in the storm," I explained. They had flown into the sky in a particularly hard downburst. Now I needed fenders to raft up alongside a boat.

"No problems," someone said. "I've got an extra one. "Here's another," a fellow sailor added. They came up with four fenders and helped me tie them on the boat.

I looked up at my newly found friends. This was a most welcome island—I had been fortunate to land among fine people.

"A sauna's good after that sail." A Canadian boater called down to me. "It'll warm you right up."

A sauna? Where was I going to find a sauna?

They pointed.

Soaked to the bone and downright shaky, I went below to find a towel and dry clothing.

My stuff had been scattered about in the storm, but I found my clothing duffel bag. I loaded my arms with clean clothing, a towel, and a dry pair of deck shoes.

When I exited the hatchway, I had difficulty standing up. The hours I spent fighting the storm took their toll on my stressed back and leg muscles. A pain throbbed in my right side, where I had been tossed against the hatchway during the knockdown. My ankle ached but was not broken as I feared. My head throbbed dully from when it smacked the bulkhead.

But all that faded when I stood on solid dry. I pulled myself upright and looked about.

Thompson Island was not large, but it had a jewel of a natural harbor set between heavily wooded hills. I glanced to the north: a hill jutted skyward, brushing aside the storm winds and protecting us in this natural refuge.

Alongside the harbor, someone had erected a wooden walkway cantilevered over the water from the rocky cliffs. The walkway circled a tree, dodged a big rock, and snaked around a cliff. Here and there were built-in rustic wooden benches. It was like somebody's sculpture garden.

My clothing squished as I walked along a wooded trail looking for the sauna. I expected something rustic, but I saw an A-frame wooden structure nestled among the pines. Smoke lazed out of the chimney. Beside the unpainted building was a pile of cut wood.

Letting my sodden clothing fall off me layer by layer, I entered the sauna. I was still shaking and unsure about all this, but I threw a dipperful of water on the sauna's hot stones and sat back on a wooden bench. Someone had stoked up the fire. Clouds of steam rose to cleanse and soothe my naked body.

I began to warm up. A remarkable sense of well-being came over me.

Whoever built a sauna on this remote barrier island certainly had good sense. They knew Superior's chill ways and how to cure them.

Greatly refreshed but wobbly, I walked back along the harbor trail and eased aboard my little boat. *Persistence* did a slight dip to welcome me. I hung my wet clothing and gear off the boom and the lifelines, where they flapped in a gentle breeze that had sprung up. The setting sun's heat beamed down on me.

My mind raced through what had happened only hours before. I did not have any good explanations: Twenty feet of wooden sailboat powered by a five-horsepower outboard had survived wild winds and high waves.

Who would believe that?

The next day, I took a brief stroll along a woodsy harbor path and found Mike Fabius, of Thunder Bay, aboard his 33-foot CS sloop, *Easy Blue.* When the storm erupted, he had been at anchor in a bay to the south of Pie Island. His son, Alistair, and four of Alistair's high school friends were on board.

"We could hear the rumbling in the background," Mike told me. The group had been ashore on the island and hurriedly returned to the boat in time to see storm clouds blocking the island's hills. "The sky turned a bright green, with some fluorescent in it. I've never seen anything like it before," Mike said.

"I thought we were secure," Mike said, "but we started dragging, and the boat was twisting sideways."

"The winds were extreme. They rotated 90 degrees."

"That was my impression, too," I said. "The wind came from two different directions."

Mike told me what happened next. The rain pounded down like stone pellets, and lightning flashed everywhere.

At the wheel, Mike sent Alistair and a teenage friend forward to the bow, but the boys couldn't get the anchor up in the high winds. Mike turned his engine to full power to ease the strain. The hook continued to drag.

"The boat was leaning at 45 degrees, and I was afraid the anchor line would snap," Mike said. "There was white spray moving horizontally several feet above the waves in 100-foot lengths, then pulling up like tails."

In between gusts, the boys finally wrestled up the hook. The skipper turned the boat downwind.

"There weren't a lot of choices," Mike said. "The waves were six to eight feet coming from two directions."

"That must have been about when I saw you," I said.

"We saw you, too. You were moving, despite the waves."

He added, "The waves were fierce."

"Any idea of the wind speed?"

"I only thought to check my anemometer *after* the worst gusts had passed. It read 72 knots." That was about 85 miles per hour.

"I heard a Mayday on the VHF earlier. A sailboat capsized. People were in the water."

"I know them. They were headed back to Thunder Bay when their sailboat got caught. Must have been some gusts coming through."

I nodded in agreement.

"Some afternoon," he said with emphasis. Yes, indeed.

Shadows fell along the harbor as I snapped on my VHF radio, called the Thunder Bay Coast Guard, and requested: "I'd like to make a long-distance telephone call."

I was trying to talk to my wife at home by radiotelephone. I suspected I was in trouble.

"So," I began carefully into the mike. "How is your Fourth of July?"

"Good," Loris answered brightly, telling me how she and our son,

Will, were getting ready to have a barbecue in the backyard. It was a hot, sultry day back in Shoreview, Minnesota.

"And how was your trip?"

"We're in an island harbor. We're OK."

I hoped I had found the right balance between telling the truth and not getting her worried. I did not want to cause her and my son pain.

There'd be time for the details to come out. Later.

"There was a report of high winds up north," she said. "Parts of Highway 61 were washed out.

"I came across a storm on the way in. But we're fine."

I tried to sound nonchalant. I ended the call: "I think we'll stick here until Superior settles down."

My original plan was to sail from Grand Portage, USA, to Silver Islet, Canada. A friend told me, "Thompson is not to be missed." And so, here I was in a tiny, wild enclave in the mouth of Thunder Cape. I learned that Thunder Bay boater Al Wray developed the harbor.

"Al was a real character who liked to party," Doug Irwin said onboard *Chris 'N Me*. Al was a World War II sailor and a battle survivor who discovered the beauties of Thompson Island after cruising the wild island archipelago guarding the mouth of Thunder Bay. "He liked it because it had a deep bay but was all natural," Doug said.

With his wife, Georgiana, and his friends, Al brought out old lumber lashed to their boats, plank by plank, and began to build the docks. They also used driftwood. When Wray died in 1985, the boaters formed a little group called Friends of Thompson Island and continued building on the island.

"They just go as they got the material," Doug said, "They stand on the dock and say, 'We can go a little more this way.' They brought out drills and rods to anchor it to the rocks, so it's environmentally friendly."

"Does the area belong to the boaters?"

"It's Crown land. It belongs to the Ontario government and is subject to its rules and regulations," Doug explained. "One is that there can be no permanent structure, but the docks are not considered a permanent structure. Neither is the sauna. And all buildings need to be unlocked and accessible to everyone.

Albert Wray is not forgotten. There's a memorial to the sailor high on the north hill overlooking the harbor.

"It's a bit of a climb, but there are ropes to assist, and there's a bench, so you can sit down and look over the harbor. Al would have loved it."

Gentle night fell early, and darkness came upon the island. I rummaged through my still-damp bilge and selected my evening's dining. Perhaps a bit of celebration was in order. Yes, it would be a can of Dinty Moore beef stew. I carefully wiped drops of lake water off the can, opened the lid, and heated the contents on my single-burner butane stove.

Dinner done, I crawled into my sleeping bag. It had been a long, eventful day, and I welcomed some warm and recuperative sack time.

I felt the boat move rhythmically in the water and began to feel myself synchronizing with the slight movements. I could hear the water lapping gently against the wooden hull.

Sometime during the night, I awoke chilled to the bone. I could not believe I could be this cold. I already wore long johns, a fleece jacket, and heavy wool socks, but I pulled on a woolen hat and piled a fleece blanket over my sleeping bag to get warm.

I had just fallen asleep again when bright flashes awakened me. I heard a powerful, jarring noise. I jumped up and put on my glasses to look out the portlight. Lightning danced about the skies to the north, illuminating the island's rocky spires.

The electrical display was followed by a great gush of wind that slammed into my boat, causing her to rock from side to side. The fenders groaned against the bigger boat to which I was rafted.

I remembered that my wet clothing hung from my cockpit lifelines and boom.

A torrent of rain fell as I threw open the dodger cover. I could feel the hard pellets slam down on my head and shoulders. I grabbed the dripping clothing and tossed it below to the cabin's floorboards. Then, after closing the canvas cover, I sat back, toweled off, and listened to the rain thumping on my cabin.

I'd been lucky. I'd have lost my clothing in the winds if the stuff hadn't been soaked and soggy. And I could not replace it.

I'd have to get a lot smarter to survive on this lake.

I began to warm up once more. My mood changed: what a fortunate person I was to be out here, in the watery world of the free—and getting smarter.

I was in the embrace of the welcome island. It encompassed me in my mind and my heart. I had escaped. ☸

PUBLICATION HISTORIES

Chapter 1: *Overboard* is excerpted from *Alone Against the Atlantic* by Gerry Spiess with Marlin Bree (Copyright Gerry Spiess and Marlin Bree). Control Data Publications 1981. **Chapter 2:** *The Lost Ships* is excerpted from *An Homage to Two Wrecks* in *Call of the North Wind* by Marlin Bree. Marlor Press, 1996. **Chapter 3:** *Raspberry* is excerpted from *Voyage to Two Islands* in *Call of the North Wind* by Marlin Bree. Marlor Press 1996. **Chapter 4:** *Ship of Death* is excerpted from *In the Waterway* in *Call of the North Wind* by Marlin Bree. Marlor Press 1996. **Chapter 5:** *The Long-Distance Cat* is excerpted from *To the Rendezvous* in *Call of the North Wind* by Marlin Bree. Marlor Press 1996. **Chapter 6:** *Gold Fever* is excerpted from *To the Gold Coast* in *In the Teeth of the Northeaster* by Marlin Bree. Marlor Press 1993. **Chapter 7:** *Isle Royale* is excerpted from *Wilderness at Isle Royale* in *In the Teeth of the Northeaster* by Marlin Bree. Marlor Press 1993. **Chapter 8:** *The Diver* is excerpted from *Rainy Day in Port* in *In the Teeth of the Northeaster* by Marlin Bree. Marlor Press 1993. **Chapter 9:** *Storm Sailor* is excerpted from *Madeline: the Enchanted Island* in *In the Teeth of the Northeaster* by Marlin Bree. Marlor Press 1993. **Chapter 10:** *The Skiff* is excerpted from *The Skiff at Port Wing* in *In the Teeth of the Northeaster* by Marlin Bree. Marlor Press 1993. **Chapter 11:** *Hollywood Comes Calling* is excerpted from *Mel Gibson's Mystery Boat* in *Wake of the Green Storm* by Marlin Bree. Marlor Press 2001. **Chapter 12:** *The Last of the Sheila Yeates* is excerpted from *The Last of the Sheila Yeates* in *Call of the North Wind* by Marlin Bree. Marlor Press 1996. **Chapter 13:** *Getting Wet* is excerpted from *To Barker's Island and Back* from *In the Teeth of the Northeaster* by Marlin Bree. Marlor Press 1993. **Chapter 14:** *The Longboat Captain* is excerpted from *To Barker's Island and Back* from *In the Teeth of the Northeaster* by Marlin bree. Marlor Press 1993. **Chapter 15:** *Storm Off the Shipwreck Coast* is excerpted from *Racing the Storm* in *Call of the North Wind* by Marlin Bree. Marlor Press 1996. **Chapter 16:** *The Shipwreck Museum* is excerpted from *Along the Shipwreck Coast* in *Call of the North Wind* by Marlin Bree. Marlor Press 1996. **Chapter 17:** *The Snowshoe Priest* is excerpted from *In the Waterway* in *Call of the North Wind* by Marlin Bree. Marlor Press 1996. **Chapter 18:** *Mystery of the Pits* is excerpted from *Mystery of the Pits* in *Wake of the Green Storm* by Marlin Bree. Marlor Press 2001. **Chapter 19:** *The Lone Racer* is excerpted from *The Passion of Mike Plant* in *Broken Seas* by Marlin Bree. Marlor Press 2005. **Chapter 20:** *Agate Island* is excerpted from *Aground!* in *Wake of the Green Storm* by Marlin Bree. Marlor Press 2001. **Chapter 21:** *The Northwoods Boatbuilder* is excerpted from *Visit to a Boatbuilder* in *Call of the North Wind* by Marlin Bree. Marlor Press 1996. **Chapter 22:** *Come Aboard!* is compiled from magazine articles by the author, including *Small Craft Advisor.* **Chapter 23:** *Amazing Gulls* is excerpted from *The Wonderful World of Gulls* in *Amazing Gulls* by Marlin Bree. Marlor Press 2011. **Chapter 24:** *Huzzah! Les Voyageurs* is excerpted from *End of the Voyage* in *In the Teeth of the Northeaster* by Marlin Bree. Marlor Press 1993. **Chapter 25:** *Secrets of Survival* is developed from several sources, including *The Day All Hell Broke Loose* in *Broken Seas* by Marlin Bree. Marlor Press 2005. **Chapter 26:** *Lure of the High Ice* is developed from a magazine article in *Cruising World.* **Epilogue:** *The Welcome Island* is excerpted from *Wake of the Green Storm* by Marlin Bree. Marlor Press 2001.

Author's Notes
Miscellaneous comments, updates and selected observations

1 | Overboard

When *Small Craft Advisor* asked me for my input on unique and innovative small boats, I nominated *Yankee Girl*. I co-wrote *Alone Against the Atlantic* with Gerry Spiess, so I knew some of the complications of the 10-footer's design and the handicaps Gerry had to overcome in such a small craft at sea. He would be one man entirely on his own resources, without outside help, so he made his boat as self-sufficient as possible to deal with problems he might encounter. Gerry tested his craft rigorously. "Don't take a new boat to sea," he told me as I built my sailboat.

Yankee Girl weighed less than 440 pounds as a bareboat, and Gerry was concerned about capsizing—going over and not coming back up. But loaded with food and supplies practically filling her cabin, she weighed 2,200 pounds, most of which he managed to stow deep in the bilge. Gerry had planned to add lead bars below, but he finally decided not to lug that extra weight. *Yankee Girl* had enough ballast—as he found out when a wave carried him overboard, and his small boat yanked him back aboard. Fully loaded when he set off for his record-breaking Atlantic voyage, Gerry joked, "I had to eat my way in." He brought back some of his extra food; I remember fondly munching on Gerry's special-recipe beef jerky. Jugs of it remained in *Yankee Girl's* bilges, except when we were writing *Alone Against the Atlantic*—when it started to disappear mysteriously.

Yankee Girl is a real sailboat: The 10-footer moves out smartly on a broad reach, but most importantly, she points high (about 45 degrees) with steadiness and speed. Gerry did not have a genoa or a spinnaker but devised a way to put up twin jibs and steer downwind with these "ponies." He learned to use these headsails on the North Atlantic, when he averaged 60 nautical miles, with a best day's run of 84 nautical miles. The speed exceeded what the *Mayflower* did on an average day's run: The Pilgrims' 100-foot ship averaged only about two nautical miles per hour and usually sailed only 48 nautical miles per day.

Gerry accomplished breakthroughs in design, construction, and small boat operations. In the grand tradition of single-handed seafaring, Gerry sailed her alone, risked everything, pitted his skills against the elements, and helmed his 10-foot boat in conditions where no one thought such a craft could survive. Today, she is well-maintained at the Minnesota Historical Society. Gerry visited her occasionally (as have I), and he told me she could still carry him on other ocean voyages. Though he designed, built, and owned various other boats, none remained so affectionately in his heart as his "little girl"—*Yankee Girl.* He missed her.

2 | The Lost Ships

In 1898, when *Pretoria's* keel was laid, boatyards were engaged in an unofficial competition to build the biggest wooden ships. On the East Coast, shipyards constructed plank-on-frame schooners with a length on deck (LOD) of 300 feet or more and reinforced by massive six- or seven-foot-high keelsons. But in heavy weather, the big schooners' wooden hulls bent and flexed, their seams opened up, and the boats leaked. All eleven of the six-masted Eastern-built large wooden vessels came to a violent end.

The *Pretoria* was similar to another giant of her day, *Wyoming.* Launched in 1909 in Bath, Maine, *Wyoming* was the last and the largest wooden six-master ever built, at 329 feet LOD. Both ships had broken the unwritten law not to build more than 300 -feet-long wooden ships. *Pretoria* was even longer at 338 feet. But Great Lakes shipbuilder James Davidson had broken with traditional schooner design and integrated pieces of steel into *Pretoria's* wooden hull. Steel plates reinforced its wooden keelson, and steel diagonal bracing

An example of the plank-on-frame construction is in the 1846 *Alvin Clark,* raised after a century underwater. Note square-headed nails. (See the chapter, *The Lost Schooner,* in *Bold Sea Stories.*)

Photo/ Dick Boyd

strapped its hull between frames. *Pretoria* also had steel cross-bracing, steel trusses, and iron arches. The steel made her stronger but also heavier.

The *Pretoria* was the final evolution in the Great Lakes schooner barge—and competitive to build since Michigan wood was plentiful, inexpensive, and easy to work with. But even with her steel reinforcing, she could not withstand a final Superior gale. The turning point had come, and shipbuilders began building all-steel boats.

The giant wooden schooners had hulls up to four feet thick, with 3- to 5-inch thick oak planking, massive ribs, and inches-thick inner planking. With massive keelsons, the wooden construction took up more cargo space than steel boats, which employed half-inch-thick steel for hull plating. Surprisingly, steel was also lighter than a wooden boat, which meant a faster ship that used less fuel. Though more expensive than wooden hulls, steel boats also proved tougher.

3 | Raspberry

Raspberry Lighthouse is one of five lighthouses in the Apostle Islands of Lake Superior, and all are viewable by boat. If you don't have a boat, you can see them from the deck of an excursion vessel out of Bayfield, Wisconsin. Raspberry is one of my favorite lighthouses, especially with historical interpreters to show visitors around. I also like the Sand Island Lighthouse (see *Bold Sea Stories,* volume 1), but when I tied up *Persistence,* I had to walk a trail through woods and swampland to get to it. A helpful Park Service lighthouse keeper pointed out where the shipwreck lay on the shoals.

4 | Ship of Death

The shipwreck of the three-masted schooner *Lucerne,* out of Ashland, Wisconsin, emphasizes Lake Superior's unpredictability, especially during late-season sailing. The big schooner dashed onto the lake with a fair weather forecast, but Superior quickly erupted in a northeaster. Three days later, the Apostle Island's lightkeeper on Long Island saw the *Lucerne's* masts protruding above the waves with three men lashed to them—frozen solid, their ship lost beneath the waves. I particularly remembered the cautionary tale of the Ship of Death as I sailed out of windswept Long Island onto the open waters of Superior for my catamaran run along the Shipwreck Coast. Even in a modern sailboat, I learned that Superior was not to be trusted.

5 | The Long-Distance Cat

When I stepped onboard *Sam,* the 31 ½-foot long catamaran of Nancy and Lyle Burke, I was especially heartened by the tale I heard. When Lyle's MS deepened, he and his wife did not stop sailing but changed from a keelboat to a catamaran and launched themselves on a 7,000-mile cruise. I particularly appreciated learning how he overcame handicaps by determination and planning (not to mention plenty of handholds). Lyle told me that Superior storms didn't bother him. "We get used to it," he said.

6 | Gold Fever

Aboard *Persistence,* I spent a night tied up near a deserted island with an underwater silver mine that was once the richest in the world (see T*he Longest Night* in *Bold Sea Stories.*). When my sailboat was temporarily berthed in a Thunder Bay marina, I drove the mesmerizing Queen's Highway on Superior's Canadian shore in search of gold. I did not find any old-time prospectors, pack mules, and pickaxes—it's all very modern these days—but I did reach the goldfields and came away with samples. (By the way, not all that glitters is gold or silver—it's the dull lead-looking stuff in silver ore, and the precious mineral doesn't even show in gold-bearing rock.) Hint: Gold and silver chunks also make good sailboat ballast and cocktail time conversation pieces when I have guests aboard.

7 | Isle Royale

This 210-square-mile island off the coast of Minnesota has become a focus for studying wolf and moose populations. At this point in history, the moose are winning. Some wolves grew weary of their island isolation (encountering tough moose) and bailed out over the winter ice into plusher grounds in Canada. These days, wildlife experts capture wolves from Superior's Canadian North Shore and fly them to the island to balance the burgeoning moose population. When I walked the island's trails, enjoying the wilderness, I peered into the tall trees but did not encounter a wolf or moose. Wildlife is secretive and smart.

8 | The Diver

After taking up SCUBA diving in Lake Superior, I found considerable interest in meeting a commercial diver in Thunder Bay. He was a hard-hat diver since he usually spent more time submerged than the SCUBA gear would allow. I took to heart his warning: "You never relax on that lake."

9 | Storm Sailor

On Madeline Island, I was honored to meet Rufus C. Jefferson, who loved to sail Superior in storms. "That's when it's the most fun," he told me. The ex-naval officer had recently returned from the Falkland Islands, the graveyard of some of the last magnificent wind ships that sailed the oceans. He was with a group trying to help bring one of the clippers back because "they're a part of our sailing heritage." Rufus planned to spend the winter on the island working on his new wooden sailboat, which he was building traditionally with planks on frames. I got to help clench nail a plank to frame, which worked well, although I decided to stick with the epoxy-saturation boatbuilding I used in *Persistence*.

10 | The Skiff

A 40-year-old rowboat hung from the roof of a storage shed, gathering dust. The White Bear Skiff was a legendary rowboat, so naturally, I had to take it for a row on Lake Superior. Its cedar planking had not swelled up, and the floorboards started to float as the hull took on water, but I got an idea of what the old-timers enjoyed. You pull on the oars in a certain way, and you glide over the water like a thing alive.

11 | Hollywood Comes Calling

In one of the remotest ports on Superior, way up north on the Canadian side, a two-decker catamaran poked its bows outside Whiskey Island. "Mel's Boat," the dock boy said knowingly. "Eh?" I asked. (Since I had been in Canada for a while, I could respond in some of the lingo.) It was a rollicking good time as the waterfront locals (and me) tried to figure out what was happening on that mega yacht. It turns out, years later, that Mel just may have been chartering that boat with his family and roaming the inland seas.

12 | The last of the *Sheila Yeates*

I was surprised when I saw a new 50-foot topsail ketch, patterned after a Civil War-era sailing vessel, appear in 1976 on Lake Superior. I got to know the captain. But after years of Superior sailing, wanderlust struck Captain Geoff Pope: he longed to sail his beloved windship across the North Atlantic. But near Greenland, *Yeates* found herself surrounded by an ice pack. A Danish trawler rammed its way to *Yeates* and began towing her, but slowly, the plank-on-frame wooden vessel tore apart and sank. Capt. Pope never stopped sailing. In his 80s, he crewed on *Cloud Nine* (skippered by Roger Swanson), rounded Cape Horn, sailed the ice of the top of the world, and circumnavigated the globe. (See the *Ice Sailor* for more on the *Cloud Nine*).

13 | Getting Wet

With a maddening amount of fresh water in front of him and a strange itch to do a little swimming, the author decides to live in a deserted boathouse along Superior and take up skin and SCUBA diving. He was pressing his luck. Hint: Dry diving suits are the warmest, especially if you wear your old armored infantry "cold war" longjohns and wool socks.

14 | The Longboat Captain

It was Capt. Guido Gulder's boathouse that I lived in when I made my solo excursions onto Superior to learn to dive. We became friends, and I learned something about this veteran longboat captain's views on the big boats, especially his thoughts on *Edmund Fitzgerald's* last hours. I had some questions because the doomed 728-foot *Fitz* never radioed a report of hitting anything. I talked with the last men in contact with the doomed *Fitz:* the captain of the following ore boat and the Duluth pilot in the salty exiting the Soo locks and entering Superior. One moment *Fitzgerald* had been in radio contact—the next, she was gone. I wondered why *Fitz* did not radio for help. It was as if the crew had not known their ship was sinking. Capt. Gulder cleared that up: "It doesn't take you long to know about a problem on a boat," he said. His ship once hit some boulders running in fog and a strong current. "What a ruckus that made," he said. "You know you hit bottom." So, yes, he felt the captain and the crew knew they hit something and were sinking— but the mystery remains.

The elderly captain and his family liked the boathouse I lived in so much that they fixed it up, enlarged it, and moved in. Years later, when I walked down the hill to the little boathouse by the water, I breathed Superior's freshwater scents. Wonderful! You only get that near the water. It brought back fond memories.

15 | Storm off the Shipwreck Coast

Helming a modern catamaran is invigorating in high winds. But our mainsail assumed a weird and tortured shape when heavy wind gusts hit. The big sail would not reef because our in-boom furler wouldn't accept the battened sail. Finally, the captain dragged the sail down and tied it around the boom. An inelegant solution, but it worked. We reefed the jib on its furler with no problems, and after that, the only way to keep going was to turn on the diesels. Later, I figured it out: the battened main would not fit into the slot atop the boom because the battens curved, and nothing we did would force them into the in-boom furler. Later, the solution came to me: I had the same problem, dropping my sailboat's main. Wind pressure made the mainsail stick in the mast's slot. All I had to do was head into the wind. The sideways pressure stopped when the sail slugs were pulled aft, and the main dropped easily onto the boom. Had we turned on the cat's diesels and motored into the wind, we would have straightened out the battens and allow the mainsail to drop easily into the in-boom furler. I decided that I did not especially appreciate in-boom furlers.

16 | The Shipwreck Museum

Thomas Farnquist started SCUBA diving in the 1970s and became obsessed with what lies beneath the dark waters along The Shipwreck Coast. His background as a science instructor shines through in educational and historical exhibits from the depths of Superior. Yes, that's a genuine relic of a lost ship—not a model or dummy. If you walk past the lighthouse, you can look out onto the big lake and peer into the distance: Out there lies the final underwater resting place of *Edmund Fitzgerald* and all its crew. Superior has an estimated 550 shipwrecks, most of which have never been found.

17 | The Snowshoe Priest

I first saw the white cross as I sailed north in my boat along the North Shore to Canada and later learned how it got there. In the 1840s, Father Frederic Baraga wanted to do the unthinkable: cross Superior's open waters in a birchbark canoe—a sometimes dangerous crossing even today in a modern boat. When they made it after fighting heavy waves and high winds, they erected a wooden cross to mark where they landed. These days, the old wooden cross is replaced by a concrete one. Baraga's cross can be reached by car along the North Shore highway. It is a scenic drive and peaceful once you arrive at the hidden cove. You might bow your head as I did.

18 | Mystery of the Pits

Historians for decades debated the meaning of the Pukaskawa Pits, but a visit to one began to unravel the mystery for me. I was on Thompson Island, and when I learned that a pit was on the island's tip, I had to check it out. We ran an inflatable to the area and walked up a rocky shore until we found it. After entering the low-lying pit, I tried sitting on the bottom and was rewarded with rocks jabbing me. Small comfort here. But ages ago, if I were "windbound" in a canoe, I could overturn my craft, get out of the wind and rain, and live in comparative ease in the wilderness. I realized once again that our boating forefathers were resourceful people.

19 | The Lone Racer

Coyote could have hit something in the water, but this seems improbable. The fin showed no signs of being crushed or struck by any object. The sides of the foil showed no signs of impact, either. Finally, the hull itself was intact and undamaged. If *Coyote* had struck a submerged object, the object would have had to have been at the same precise depth as *Coyote's* bulb. Ominously, the Coast Guard report concluded: "It appears that the only submerged object that struck *Coyote's* keel bulb was the muddy bottom of the Chesapeake Bay." Mike had gotten his boat stuck in the mud and had tried to twist the keel free.

The report analyzed the design and construction of *Coyote's* keel and ballast bulb. With her draft of roughly 14 feet, Coyote's hull drew 1 foot 3 inches of water. Her fin was 11-feet-2-inches-deep and only 45 inches long. Below the fin's bottom hung the 18-inch deep, 8,400-pound lead ballast bulb. The ballast bulb was fastened on a 31-inch long main keel assembly. This gave the 112-inch-long-bulb enormous, deadly leverage upon a short keel span as *Coyote* pounded through heavy weather. In the racer's drive across the stormy ocean, the fin must have had tremendous forces twisting on it.

The foil emanated a humming noise and a vibration that Mike felt and heard during tests. So did the crewmembers he had aboard during tests. But looking through *Coyote's* bottom sight glass while underway, no one could observe any movement of the keel or bulb as the vessel worked in the seas.

The Coast Guard focused on *Coyote's* two groundings in the mud of Chesapeake Bay. The efforts to free the vessel while it was struck in the bottom "resulted in the bulb being twisted and dragged through the mud. The twisting and dragging of the bulb, and the shifting of the vessel's weight across the keel, most likely weakened the 31-inch joint that fastened the bulb to the foil."

Though the fin keel survived the capsize and was recovered with *Coyote,* only the ballast bulb was missing. The Coast Guard noted that "there was virtually no significant damage to the *Coyote* other than the fact that the bulb was missing." The Coast Guard concluded that "the loss of *Coyote's* keel bulb was a failure of the carbon fiber materials used to secure the 8,400-pound bulb assembly to the base of the keel's foil. When the material failed, the bulb assembly—including the lead bulb, the keel bolts, and the stainless steel plate—dropped off the keel, and *Coyote* capsized."

If Mike had been uninjured and able to stay with his boat, or if he had been pitched in the water and able to swim back to *Coyote* after the capsize, she would have sheltered him. Her bottom floated high out of the water on five airtight chambers, and there would have been more than sufficient air below to live under. Probably he could have fashioned the underside of a bunk to keep him out of the water, just as other survivors of capsizes had done. He had provisions and survival gear on board.

The report added: "Had he survived for a period of time afterward, he would have remained with the vessel and marked the hull in some fashion to indicate he was inside—such as putting a rag through the sight glass in the hull. He also would have tethered the EPIRB to the vessel to prevent it from drifting away and inflated the life raft to be able to get out of the water.

The Coast Guard concluded: "Mike Plant probably was killed when the vessel capsized."

On January 26, 1993, *Coyote* was again located on the North Atlantic. She had drifted about 60 miles south and west of the Irish coast. The tug, *Ventenor,* secured towing lines to her foil and both rudders. Ignobly, *Coyote* was towed stern first to Ireland.

She was hauled aboard a freighter for a trans-Atlantic trip back to the U.S. Incredibly, after months adrift on the open Atlantic, she was pronounced sound after extensive ultrasound testing. She was rebuilt by designer Rodger Martin, who added an interior skeleton of carbon fiber tubing for additional stiffness. *Coyote* got a more streamlined deckhouse, a bowsprit, and a reconfigured rig to carry even more sail area. She also received a new keel and bulb.

The racer lost about 1,000 pounds in her rebuild and got even faster. In the 1994 -95 BOC race, she circled the globe with David Scully as her skipper and came in fourth. *Coyote* scored an admirable total time of 133 days, 56 minutes, and 35 seconds, averaging 8.21 knots. She placed second in her class in the 1996 Europe One Star Transatlantic Race.

Mike's family established the Mike Plant Fund at the Minnetonka Yacht Club to help underprivileged children learn the joys of sailing in the same waters that Mike sailed as a boy.

In 2002, in a ceremony held in Newport, Mike Plant was inducted into the Museum of Yachting's Single Handed Sailor's Hall of Fame. His friend, Herb McCormick, said at the dedication ceremonies: "One of the great tragedies of Mike's passing is the awful timing. Here he was, finally, after three circumnavigations, truly ready to contend for the crown. If all went well, if he had that mix of luck and execution required of all champions, he was ready to challenge the best on his own terms. He was ready to live his biggest dream."

20 | Agate Island

You can pick lovely little purple rocks off the beach. What a treasure hunt—if you're up to getting there by boat past The Island of Doom and Mystery Island and a few hundred unmarked reefs. But then you arrive at Agate Island. What's that between your toes? A purple-colored pebble—an agate? You're rich. Well, maybe not.

21 | The Northwoods Boatbuilder

Many colorful waterfront characters live along the shores of Lake Superior and Michigan's wooded shores. As I cruised the Shipwreck Coast, I met a wonderful boatbuilder with a sense of humor. "I only work half days," he told me straight-faced. "Eight to eight, always 12 hours—that's only half a day. It's only a part-time job." The Bingham Boat Works builds sturdy, seaworthy boats, and I found it helpful to listen to how Joe feels a proper Lake Superior boat should be put together. Hint: None of Joe's boats had a fin keel.

22 | Come Aboard!

There's adventure aboard a sailboat. As the wind fills our sails and we shove off on a blustery day, you can get an idea of what I like in a boat, including the well-tuned tiller, balanced rudder blade, the location of the mid-cockpit traveler, the use of the backstay adjuster, and playing the traveler in gusts. I'll bet you won't think about the office, either.

23 | Amazing Gulls

The sailors' friends often don't get much respect. Yet, with their distinctive v-shaped, high aspect ratio wings, they're wind machines worthy of study and interest. They fly exceedingly well, glide endlessly, and hover in thermals. In some tourist areas of Superior, notably in Duluth, the gulls have become a waterfront attraction, with children throwing bread crumbs in the air for the acrobatic gulls to catch. There's still a mystery about how they know where to fly thousands of miles south each year, sometimes as far as Mexico or South America. And return the following year.

24 | Huzzah! Les Voyagers

"You're about the right size for a voyageur," a fur trading post guide told me. It was a compliment of sorts, for although I am not a tall guy, I am muscular from boat-building and sailing. Yet when I tried to lift just one fur bundle that voyageurs carried in the wilderness—I could not do it more than a few inches. It weighed 90 pounds. The voyageurs, who paddled out of New France in birchbark canoes, could carry several of these on their 36 portages between Montreal and Grand Portage—the very edge of civilization 200 years ago. Voyageurs were renowned for their strength, stamina (paddling their canoes from dawn to dusk), and cheerful manner. I followed the historic wake of the canoe brigades on my route in *Wake of the Green Storm.*

25 | Secrets of Survival

In winds estimated at 134 mph., my boat was tossed about. But I survived the Green Storm, as the July 4, 1999 Derecho came to be known, and in this chapter, I relate some of the tactics and maneuvers that let me and my boat survive. Hint: the boat did most of the work. I mostly just hung on. I sometimes think back to the several-hour delay I encountered while waiting for my damp outboard to start and the fog to lift. Had I begun my voyage to Thompson Island a little sooner, I would have been in the island's harbor and sheltered from the storm. After I returned from my voyage, I designed and sewed up a Sunbrella cover to encapsulate the outboard's power head. The cover shades the engine from the heat of the day and keeps the powerhead dry during rainstorms and heavy fog. I think it helps.

26 | Lure of the High Ice

I met Roger Swanson when we spoke at a sailing club in Minneapolis, and I soon learned I was in the presence of a world-class sailor and adventurer. Roger told me he was fifty when he began his long-distance voyaging career in earnest: He bought a 57-foot Bowman Ketch and started sailing. A short trip turned into a 28-month trip around the world. He sailed around the world three times and put over 217,000 nautical miles under *Cloud Nine's* wake, The lure of high ice beckoned, and he became the first skipper of an American sailboat to cross the fabled Northwest Passage from east to west in a year.

Was he ever frightened? Roger told me he never had time to be scared in an emergency—he was too busy. He advised sailors who'd like to cruise: "If you want to go cruising, do it. If I had waited until I had the time and could afford it, I wouldn't have left Minnesota."

Herb McCormick, the senior editor of *Cruising World,* called him "one of the greatest long-distance voyagers of this era or any other era. Few sailors have gone from the Arctic to the Antarctic and everywhere in between. He was one of a kind."

ACKNOWLEDGMENTS

People who helped this book come alive

A book such as this results from many people's energies and skills, and I am grateful for their help. I wish to thank Theresa Gedig, of DigDesign, for her design of the cover and the inside pages and for contributing all the many graces a graphic designer can lend in creatively developing a manuscript into a finished book. Pat Morris, a former editor for *Good Old Boat,* brought her skills in editing the rough manuscript and helped polish up my prose. It is surprising what a good editor can do. Boating Writers International was a great source of information and sharing. Every boating writer should belong to this professional organization. I also appreciate the help and counsel of the Author's Guild, which hosts my home page and books at **www.marlinbree.com.** Some of the magazines I contributed to were helpful in helping me run down leads and information, including *Small Craft Advisor* and editor Josh Colvin; *The Ensign* (magazine of the U.S. Power Squadron), with editor Yvonne Hill at the helm; and *Cruising World,* the distinguished editor and sailor Herb McCormick providing information, especially on the Mike Plant Story. *Lake Superior* magazine is a source of illumination and mutual concern, with editor Kon LeMay running the editorial side. I especially want to thank Bruce Lynn at the Great Lakes Shipwreck Museum, who so ably carries on the work and the vision of the Museum's founder, Thomas Farnquist.

Helping in many ways with the manuscript was Judy Swanholm. Thanks, Judy. Keep up your excellent work with Guthrie. A notable supporter is Thom Mathisen of Northern Lights Sailing Club. In Canada, I always felt I could rely on Clive Dudley of Thunder Bay, Ontario, and "The Island Gang." Lastly, I'd like to thank Will Bree, my son, for his support during the writing process, including many midnight writing hours.

Marlin Bree

Marlin Bree sailing the *Persistence*

Art/Marlin Bree

About the Author

Marlin Bree is an award-winning marine journalist and the author of many boating books, including *In the Teeth of the Northeaster*, *Wake of the Green Storm*, the *Boat Log & Record*, *Dead on the Wind*, and *Broken Seas*. He co-authored *Alone Against the Atlantic* with Gerry Spiess. His books are sold in bookstores, internet booksellers, and marine distributors. Marlin's books are distributed to the book trade in the United States by IPG Books, Chicago, and are available in trade paperback form, e-books, and as pdf's. Some are available as audiobooks. He is a member of Boating Writers International and The Author's Guild. His website, **www.marlinbree.com**, contains details and photos of the author's home-built boat, *Persistence*, and shows some of his boat building and maintenance tips. Also shown in color are scenic locations in which the author has sailed *Persistence*.

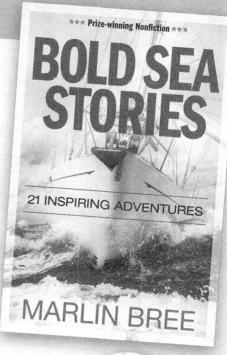

Made in United States
North Haven, CT
14 September 2023

41530380R00124